HRM from A–Z

Critical Questions Asked & Answered

Christopher L. Martin
Louisiana State University in Shreveport

Roland E. Kidwell, Jr.
Niagara University

McGraw-Hill
Irwin

Boston   Burr Ridge, IL   Dubuque, IA   Madison, WI   New York
San Francisco   St. Louis   Bangkok   Bogotá   Caracas   Kuala Lumpur
Lisbon   London   Madrid   Mexico City   Milan   Montreal   New Delhi
Santiago   Seoul   Singapore   Sydney   Taipei   Toronto

McGraw-Hill Higher Education

A Division of The McGraw-Hill Companies

HRM FROM A-Z
Published by McGraw-Hill/Irwin, an imprint of The McGraw-Hill Companies, Inc. 1221
Avenue of the Americas, New York, NY, 10020. Copyright © 2001, by The McGraw-Hill Companies, Inc. All rights reserved. No part of this publication may be reproduced or distributed in any form or by any means, or stored in a data base or retrieval system, without the prior written consent of The McGraw-Hill Companies, Inc., including, but not limited to, in any network or other electronic storage or transmission, or broadcast for distance learning.
Some ancillaries, including electronic and print components, may not be available to customers outside the United States.

This book is printed on acid-free paper.

1 2 3 4 5 6 7 8 9 0 QPD/QPD 0 9 8 7 6 5 4 3 2 1 0

ISBN   0-07-246599-9

Vice president and editor-in-chief: *Robin J. Zwettler*
Publisher: *John E. Biernat*
Senior editor: *John Weimeister*
Editorial assistant: *Trina Hauger*
Senior marketing manager: *Ellen Cleary*
Project manager: *Destiny Rynne*
Production supervisor: *Debra R. Sylvester*
Coordinator freelance design: *Mary Kazak*
Cover design: *AM Design*
Compositor: *Carlisle Communications, Ltd.*
Printer: *Quebecor World Dubuque Inc.*

Library of Congress Card Number: 00-110535

www.mhhe.com

Contents

Answers

TOPIC AREA	TREATED IN	TOPIC AREA	TREATED IN
Legal Context of Employment Decisions	"Alcohol abuse" "Family concerns" "FMLA" "Health inquiries" "Height & weight" "Hygiene" "Interview questions" "Language restrictions" "Military leave" "Older workers" "Pregnant employees" "Religion & Muzak®" "Religious holidays" "Romance" "Sexual harassment" "Tongue rings & tatoos"	**Orientation & Training**	"Adult learners" "Change" "Empowerment" "Family concerns" "HRM" "Strategy and" "Tokenism"
		Diversity	"Adult learners" "Casual clothing" "Diversity" "Hygiene" "Language restrictions" "Older workers" "Tokenism" "Tongue rings & tattoos" "'X' generation"
Job Analysis & Planning	"Independent contractor" "Job descriptions" "Key job responsibilities" "Natural attrition" "Promotion from within" "Succession planning"	**Quality & Productivity**	"Complaints & excuses" "Corporate culture" "Emotions & expressing opinions" "Empowerment" "Gossip" "Group conflict" "Key job responsibilities" "Learning organization" "Quality management during downsizing" "'Slackers'"
Recruiting	"Expatriate manager" "Independent contractor" "Promotion from within" "Religion & Muzak®" "Theft & forgiveness" "Turnover" "Work relationships"		
		Managing Careers	"Gender & leadership" "Job hopping" "Older workers" "Performance feedback & career development" "Promotion to management" "Repatriation" "Romance" "Succession planning" "Tuition reimbursement"
Selection & Placement	"Accidents" "Diversity" "Drug testing" "Expatriate manager" "Health inquiries" "Height & weight" "Honesty tests" "Interview questions" "Personality conflicts" "Reference checks" "Team building" "Violence" "Work relationships"		
		Developing Managers	"Jokes & humor" "Leadership style" "Learning organization" "Micro-management" "Promotion to management" "Succession planning" "X & Y management"
Unions & Labor Relations	"'Salting'" "Union comfort level" "'Yellow dog' contracts"		

TOPIC AREA	TREATED IN	TOPIC AREA	TREATED IN
Pay systems	"Beepers" "Commission sales" "Dating clients" "Incentives" "Money as a motivator" "Overtime" "Pay secrecy" "Turnover"	**International HRM** **H Health & Safety**	"Expatriate manager" "Family concerns" "Kidnapping" "Repatriation" "Xenophobia" "Accidents" "Alcohol abuse"

Benefits & Services	"Absenteeism"
	 "Alcohol abuse"
	 "Battered & abused
	  coworker"
	 "FMLA"
	 "Health plan alternatives"
	 "Napping at work"
	 "Nosy boss"
	 "Religious holidays"
	 "Sick leave banks"
	 "Tuition reimbursement"
	 "Unemployment
	  compensation"
	 "Weather, storms,
	  & natural disasters"
		
		 Strategic HRM
			"Alcohol &
			  the office party"
			 "Battered & abused
			  coworker"
			 "Fetal protection policy"
			 "Gambling"
			 "OSHA audits"
			 "Napping at work"
			 "Smokers"
			 "Violence at work"
			
			 "Casual clothing"
			 "Corporate culture"
			 "Job-hopping"
			 "Learning organization"
			 "Strategy & HRM"
			 "'X'-generation"
			 "Zero-defects"

Appraising Performance	"Complaints & excuses"
	 "Dating clients"
	 "Discipline"
	 "Performance evaluation &
	  the angry employee"
	 "Performance feedback &
	  career development"		

Fairness, Ethics, & Employee Relations	"Absenteeism" "Beepers, pagers" "Belligerence" "Discipline" "E-mail use/abuse" "Employment-at-will" "Gambling" "Hygiene" "Internet use/abuse" "Off-duty conduct" "Privacy & HRIS" "Smokers" "Soliciting" "Theft prevention"		

Preface

The questions and answers in *HRM from A to Z: Critical Questions Asked & Answered* originated in 1994 as a monthly newspaper column entitled *Management Matters*, which continues to be published six years and over 100 questions later. We started the column by soliciting questions about management issues from local managers and employees and from our working MBA and undergraduate students. Since the column began, we have revisited original questions and answers and updated them to reflect changes in law or human resource management practices that have occurred over the last few years. The questions in this book reflect concerns posed to us from practitioners, business owners, managers, and employees. They also reflect trends that we have noticed in the rapidly changing HRM environment, particularly in strategic and global human resource management.

Each question in this book is listed alphabetically by a guide word or phrase that indicates the major issue. The question pages include key words and concepts, discussion points, and a suggested reference. The key words and suggested references are provided to give the students a starting point in researching their answers to the questions. The discussion points are designed to assist the instructor in using the questions as practical examples of theoretical material that is covered in most introductory human resource management courses. Thus, we see this book as a means to introduce practical application into HRM topic areas such as staffing, training and development, performance appraisal, and reward systems.

In the second part of the book, we have offered answers to each of the questions posed along with a few additional references. We don't pretend that our answers are comprehensive or the only possible way to answer the question, but we provide them as a starting point for continued research. We also don't assert that our references are exhaustive, but that they represent only a handful of places where more information about the topic might be obtained.

We hope that as you—the student—use this book, you will raise questions about our answers, suggest answers of your own, and go beyond what is here to more fully address the continually evolving area of human resource management. Please contact us with suggestions and criticisms of our work. The easiest way is by e-mail: cmartin@pilot.lsus.edu or rek@niagara.edu. We thank you for your interest and hope you enjoy the book.

To the students and the instructor: How to use this book

HRM from A to Z : Critical Questions Asked & Answered is designed as a supplemental text in an introductory human resource management course or graduate HRM seminar. We have used the questions in the book to help our undergraduate and graduate students focus on practical applications of theoretical approaches to HRM, which are the standard elements of a general text. Thus, the instructor may want to assign a question or two in the book before, or just after, lecturing on a topic area such as employment law or recruiting. The students can use the interim between classes to prepare their answers to the question and the discussion points. Following a concept lecture, the assigned questions can then be used to spark interest in the students to take part in a class discussion that focuses on a real HRM problem.

Aside from forming the basis for class discussion, another way to use the questions is as a group project assignment. For example, the authors have formed student groups to research questions and provide their suggested responses to the question and the discussion points. The students who were not presenting were asked to read the question in conjunction with material from the main text and take part in class discussion following the presentation. The student teams found this exercise extremely worthwhile because it honed their research skills and enabled them to connect theory to practical problems and solutions. The answers suggested by the students after their research added value to the answers that had already been provided by the authors.

One issue with this book is its presentation of the suggested answers only a few pages away from the questions. Students who are assigned questions to research should go beyond the suggested answer offered in the book, or preferably not look at the book's answer until they complete their research. Realizing the difficulty of that temptation, it may be worthwhile for the instructor to ask that the student researchers obtain additional references beyond those offered on the answer pages, to ask the students to examine the suggested answer for flaws, and/or to assign the students to identify a web site related to the issue and provide information from that site for class discussion.

The questions in this book also might serve as the basis for practical application questions on HRM exams. In some instances, the authors have reformulated the questions into multiple-choice exam or short essay questions to test the linkage students are able to make from theory to practice. As a student, you may have an opinion as to whether this will help you master basic material in an HRM course. The questions and answers herein may help you to clarify your ideas for an HRM research paper.

At any rate, the way this book is used is limited only by the imagination of the students and their instructors. We hope you have as much success in connecting concept to practice as our students have in working with earlier versions of this product.

Christopher L. Martin, Ph.D.
Louisiana State University in Shreveport

Roland E. Kidwell, Jr., Ph.D.
Niagara University

A

Absenteeism

? I need advice on how to deal with an abuse of sick time. One of our employees asked her supervisor for permission to attend a two-day, company-sponsored workshop that she felt would benefit her. The supervisor disagreed with the benefits, stated that he was too understaffed to allow her to attend, and denied her request. She persisted and asked for vacation time so she could attend. She had previously taken all of her vacation time when this request was made. The supervisor denied additional vacation time and his decision was supported by the department head. Rather than taking "No" for the answer, the employee took four days of sick leave and attended two days of the workshop. The supervisor now wants to start disciplinary procedures based on abuse of our sick leave policy. To complicate matters further, the employee has a note from her doctor excusing her absences from work during the entire four-day period for "stress-related" reasons. The note did not specify the cause of her stress, but I'll bet she'll somehow tie it back to the job. What potential problems could we face when or if we discipline the employee? Our policy prohibits the misuse of sick time and allows for discipline up to and including termination.

Key Words / Concepts: job satisfaction, stress-related illness, discipline, absenteeism, employee development

Discussion Points: What are alternatives to the use of discipline as a means to force employees to show up to work? How do working conditions play a role in absences? How might a company determine if absenteeism is related to a particular supervisor's inappropriate management style or manner?

Related Reference: Tyler, Kathryn (1997). Dependability can be a rewarding experience. *HRMagazine*, December, Vol.42, No.12, p.57-60.

Accidents

It seems as if 95 percent of the accidents in my shop are caused by 5 percent of my employees. I have what I feel is a very strong safety program in my facility. However, my accident-prone 5 percent and their workers' compensation claims are going to run me out of business. Do you have any suggestions?

Key Words / Concepts: workplace safety, accident-prone people, Americans with Disabilities Act (ADA), unsafe acts, unsafe conditions, workers' compensation, accidents

Discussion Points: How much should employers ask about an applicant's safety record and previous injuries during the job interview? Other than asking the applicant directly about a previous record, how might relevant information to reduce on-the-job injuries be obtained?

Related Reference: Insel, Paul M. (1997). Accident prone or unsafe behavior. *Healthline*, December, p.6-7.

Adult learners

Last year, I was appointed the safety manager at our company, a chemical manufacturer. On Wednesdays, I meet with employees for an hour to go over important safety matters that they need to know to perform their jobs without getting injured. I usually go to a lot of trouble and prepare very detailed slide shows on PowerPoint. I had been doing this training for a couple of months when I found out from one of the line managers that the employees were not following the new procedures I had presented to them. When I asked one of the men privately why they were not following my instructions, he said, "You've been treating us like a bunch of kids and we're bored to tears." I knew going in that this group would likely have a short attention span. However, I thought the use of PowerPoint would overcome it. Can you give me some ideas on why they might have reacted in this manner and what I should do in the future?

Key Words / Concepts: andragogy, multimedia, learning theory, social learning, training, adult learning

Discussion Point: Is the safety manager the best person to provide safety training? How might a presentation tool like PowerPoint enhance learning? Hinder learning?

Related Reference: Wolfson, James W. (1997). Improving adult performance in business education. *Business Education Forum*, December, p.18-21.

Alcohol abuse

One of my best managers came back to the office from lunch and was obviously "bombed." He was slurring his speech, his face was bright red, and I could smell alcohol on his breath, along with the chips and hot sauce from lunch. His behavior was an embarrassment to me and to the company. I was ready to pull him in my office and let him have it when a colleague warned me that if I reprimanded him in any way and brought up his alcohol problem, I could be in violation of the ADA. The material she showed me seemed to back her position. Are we missing something? By the way, we're a small company and don't have a specific written policy on this.

Key Words / Concepts: substance abuse, Americans with Disabilities Act (ADA), employee assistance program (EAP), alcohol and drug testing

Discussion Points: Should employee use of alcohol on the job be an automatic firing offense? Why or why not? Under what circumstances should employers test employees for alcohol use? Would a test be necessary to take action in the case described here?

Related Reference: Bahles, Jane E. (1999). Handle with care. *HRMagazine*, March, Vol. 44, No.3, p.60-66.

Alcohol & the office party

We are preparing for our annual Christmas party and have run into a snag. This morning, when our planning committee got together, one of our new managers went berserk over the idea of providing alcohol to the employees. We have always had an open bar and have never run into any problems. He argued that because the company is sponsoring the function, we would be liable for any accidents or injuries that occurred at the party or on the way home from the party. He claims no one serves alcohol anymore because you can't defend the claims. I realize we're a lawsuit happy society, but surely it hasn't come to this.

Key Words / Concepts: liability insurance, contributory negligence, work team cohesiveness

Discussion Points: Should companies have a specific alcohol policy regarding office parties? If a company would take disciplinary action against employees for drinking at work at other times, does serving alcohol at the Christmas party send the wrong message? Would serving alcohol hurt morale among those who do not drink?

Related Reference: Solomon, Robert & Usprich, Sydney (1993). Being sued can ruin a good party. *Business Quarterly*, Spring Vol.57, No.3, p.53-63.

B

Battered & abused coworker

I work as an office manager in a small office and supervise about eight other women. Last week one of my employees came to work with two black eyes, which she attempted to hide with make-up. This isn't the first time she's come in late (and bruised) or not come in at all. The other girls volunteered that she had a fight with her boyfriend and he hit her. I don't want to see one of my employees getting abused, but I'm not sure how to handle this one.

Key Words / Concepts: domestic violence, workplace violence, employee privacy, employee assistance program (EAP), community services

Discussion Points: What are the interests of the office manager, the employee, and the company in this situation? How do you balance the interests of each?

Related Reference: Woodward, Nancy, H. (1998). Domestic abuse policies in the workplace. *HR Magazine*, Vol.43, No.6, May, p.116-123.

Beepers, pagers, & cell phones

? I was given a beeper by my company a few months ago so I could be reached in case of an emergency. Now everything at work has become an emergency, according to my boss and my employees. They constantly page me at night, on weekends, even during Game 6 of the NBA finals when I was at a bar. I feel like I have no privacy left with this constant badgering about every trivial detail, even matters that don't even relate to work. It's not like I'm a doctor or anything. I'm the operations director of a building supply company. We're closed on Sundays, but I still get beeped. What can I do about this?

Key Words / Concepts: electronic monitoring, Electronic Communications Privacy Act, employee privacy rights, telecommunications, on-call policy

Discussion Points: What kind of balance can be struck between the need to contact key employees and allowing them privacy from being contacted away from the job? Should the company inform employees that the paging system is subject to employer monitoring? Should use of a paging system be limited to business communication? Why or why not?

Related Reference: Hirschman, Carolyn (1999). Paying for waiting. *HRMagazine*, August, Vol.44, No.8, p.98-103.

Belligerence

? I'm the personnel director at a company of about 100 employees. Recently, the president of the company and I called a meeting with the employees to try to improve communication in the plant. We told the employees to come with questions and to say what was on their minds. About 20 employees showed up.

Fifteen minutes into the meeting, an employee named Joe started berating the president and complaining that an employee had received a big raise not to quit the company while another employee—a friend of Joe's—was not given more money to stay. I tried to say his complaint was not true, but he told me not to interrupt until he was finished. Joe went on for about 15 minutes saying that management could not be trusted and calling me and the president liars even after we explained his allegations about the pay raises were not true. Basically, after he had finished, the time set aside for the meeting was over.

I was so steamed about this situation that I want to fire Joe for attacking my boss and me at this meeting. He embarrassed us in front of several employees. I don't think it was appropriate for him to bring up pay issues involving specific employees and I certainly think he was insubordinate for attacking us the way he did. The president doesn't want to fire Joe for attacking us. What do you think we should do?

Key Words / Concepts: communication, facilitation, grapevine, pay secrecy, fairness in discipline, insubordination, guaranteed fair treatment, opinion surveys, speak-up programs, top-down programs

Discussion Points: How might this company have used various communication strategies to avoid what occurred at this meeting? Should Joe be fired? Why or why not?

Related Reference: Ash, Stephen (1996). Coping with personal disputes and defense of employees: how to play the role of mediator at work. *Manage*, July, Vol.48, No.1, p.28-29.

C

Casual clothing

Now that the weather is warming up, my employees have been hounding me more than ever to let them shed the suits and ties for more casual office wear. Although I know a lot of companies have been going this route, I'm not sold. Isn't this change to casual dress occurring more in manufacturing-type companies, like our local GM plant, where there is little contact with customers? Whatever happened to the idea of "dressing for success"?

Key Words / Concepts: employee dress codes, employee uniforms, sex discrimination

Discussion Points: How important is an organization's culture to its decision to allow casual dress at work? Should a company that allows casual dress post a notice to alert customers so they will not be surprised or offended? If you visited a company, as a potential customer, and the company's employees dressed casually to meet with you but you dressed up in formal business attire, would this lessen your desire to do business with that company?

Related Reference: Mannix, Margaret (1997). Casual Friday, five days a week. *U.S. News & World Report*, August 4, Vol.123, No.5, p.60.

Change

Roy has been a solid, dependable employee in my small, machine shop for the last 20 years. Recently, we modernized the machinery in the operation where Roy works. This change means that Roy will have to learn how to use new equipment, for the first time since he's been with us. He is very upset about having to develop these new skills, and I'm concerned that I may have to let him go. Do you have any suggestions as to why he's acting this way and if there is anything we can do about it?

Key Words / Concepts: on-the-job training, vestibule training, resistance to change, technological change

Discussion Points: How could co-workers help with this situation? Will there be problems with discrimination laws if Roy is fired for refusing to work with the new equipment?

Related Reference: Greengard, Samuel (1998). How technology will change the workplace. *Workforce*, January, Vol.77, No.1, p.78-84.

Commission sales

We will be adding a new telecommunications marketing/sales position to our organization within the next six months. My company would like to pay the individual who will be hired for this slot a percent of gross sales to keep incentive high. What are your thoughts?

Key Words / Concepts: reward systems, pay for performance, incentives, compensation strategies

Discussion Points: Which types of jobs lend themselves to commission sales? Are there particular sales jobs in which incentives would be inappropriate? Incentive systems seem like a good thing; discuss possible negatives.

Related Reference: Halverson, Richard (1992). Sears nixes commission pay in light of fraud charges. *Discount Store News*, July 6, Vol.31, No.13, p.7.

Complaints & excuses

 I work in an office with a person named Frank who is constantly complaining about how overworked he is, how he can barely keep up with the jobs he's given, and how much his back aches each day.   When I ask him for something I need, there's always an excuse for why I got it late, or not at all.

It's often been easier for me to do it myself, rather than to deal with his excuses and to listen to the moaning. Now I find myself picking up an even greater share of the load. Because I've "done such a good job," I get picked by the boss to do all sorts of special projects, and Frank gets picked for nothing. I'm at the office working late, and he's out the door at 5 P.M. I don't think the situation is fair, but I don't want the boss to think I'm not a team player. In addition, if I get him fired, they'll probably give me the rest of his work. What can I do?

Key Words / Concepts: performance standards, halo effect, critical incident method, impression management, supervisor observation

Discussion Points: Identify some of the reasons why Frank may be doing what he is perceived as doing. If you were Frank and you read this question, how would you explain yourself?

Related Reference: Becker, Thomas E. & Martin, Scott L. (1995). Trying to look bad at work: Methods and motives for managing poor impressions in organizations. *Academy of Management Journal*, Vol.38, p.174-199.

Corporate culture

 Prior to my arrival in this company, all decisions were handled in a very top-down manner. Decisions were always conservative and if a problem was to

arise, you always checked with the boss first before any action was taken. Even though we have been the market leader for years, I know that if we want to continue to be "number 1," we've got to act faster and take a few more risks. However, during the past year I've been unable to get the people in my organization to get off their butts, take some risks, and be innovative. Any suggestions?

Key Words / Concepts: change, taking risks, innovation

Discussion Points: What factors should be considered when an organization is attempting to change its culture? What incentives do members of successful organizations have to change culture? How might organizational culture change take place?

Related Reference: Bozeman, B. & Kingsley, G. (1998). Risk culture in public and private organizatons. *Public Administration Review*, March-April, Vol.58, No.2, p.109-118.

D

Dating clients

? I'm a sales manager at a very aggressive industrial company. Members of our sales force have always been pitted against each other to increase volume ever upward. This has apparently created a problem involving my one female salesperson, who has become a top performer at the company after only a year on the job. Last week, one of my customers phoned and told me that "Jennifer" is sleeping with several of her key clients. One of my salesmen confirmed she was dating at least one customer and used this as an excuse as to why he was unable to match her sales. What should I do?

Key Words / Concepts: policies, relevant performance criteria, sexual harassment, sex discrimination, workforce demographics

Discussion Points: What is the most important problem here? Does it involve legal or company performance issues, or both?

Related Reference: Powell, Gary N. & Foley, Sharon (1998). Something to talk about: Romantic relationships in organizational settings. *Journal of Management*, Vol.24, p.421-448.

Discipline

Recently, one of my co-workers was trying to help a customer when another lady tapped her on the shoulder and asked for help. My co-worker said, "If you'll wait just a second, I will be glad to help you." When she was finished helping the first customer, she turned to the second customer. By then the lady was infuriated and said my co-worker was terrible at her job and started insulting her. The co-worker apologized, but the insults continued. The co-worker lost her cool and used a racial slur toward the customer. About 15 people witnessed the incident, which was reported to the supervisor. No disciplinary action has been taken against my co-worker. Meanwhile, our work group—which is racially mixed—has suffered a drop in morale because of this incident and the lack of punishment. What should the supervisor have done?

Key Words / Concepts: racial discrimination, hot stove rule, progressive discipline, self-discipline, workforce diversity

Discussion Point: Could anything have been done in the training of either the employee or the supervisor to avoid this situation?

Related Reference: Bielous, Gary A. (1993). How to discipline effectively. *Supervision*, April, Vol. 54, No.4, p.17-19.

Diversity

A new manager recently transferred to our local office from up north and works under me supervising the hourly employees. In the two months since he arrived, "Jim" has managed to alienate the office staff with his abrupt and rude Yankee style of management. I brought him down here because he is extremely qualified so far as the knowledge and skills to do the job, but in the interview I didn't realize he could be so abrasive. What can I do to help him fit in?

Key Words / Concepts: knowledge, skills, and abilities (KSA); values; personality; selection tests; interviewing

Discussion Points: Is being a Yankee in the South a diversity issue? How much of this situation is Jim's fault versus the office staff and Jim's supervisor? Why? How does a manager conduct an interview in order to find out about the manners of the job applicant?

Related Reference: Capowski, Genevieve (1998). Can't see the diversity for all the differences. *HR Focus*, July, Vol.75, No.7, p.16.

Drug testing

Although my company hasn't had any problems with drugs in the workplace, we are considering pre-employment drug screening. We hire a lot of high school and college age kids. So, in a conversation with my teenage son and his friends, I told them about our plan and asked them how they would feel if they were required to provide a urine sample at a job interview. None of them said they'd feel it was an invasion of privacy, which was my concern. However, they did say we were wasting our time because everybody knows that drug tests can be easily faked. One of the kids even showed me a company on the Internet selling a product guaranteed to give you "clear and clean" test results. It's ridiculous that a product like this is available. What can be done? If the tests can be compromised so easily, they hardly seem worth the expense and trouble.

Key Words / Concepts: pre-employment drug testing, random drug testing, privacy

Discussion Points: Contrast a local company's approach to illegal drugs with its approach to legal drugs such as tobacco and alcohol. What should the similarities and differences be?

Related Reference: Bahls, Jane Easter (1998). Dealing with drugs: Keep it legal *HRMagazine*, March, Vol.43, No.3, p.104-111.

E

E-mail use/abuse

A friend of mine recently got
lambasted by his boss for "e-mail abuse."
Ron sent a private e-mail to a colleague who
called into question the boss's leadership . . . or lack thereof.
Ron was told that his e-mail, other employees' e-mail, and all
Internet activities were being monitored. He was told to stay off nonbusiness-related
websites and to keep his personal gripes off the e-mail. This certainly seems like an
invasion of an employee's rights.

Key Words / Concepts: employee monitoring, electronic monitoring, privacy

Discussion Points: Is this an unusual practice? Can Ron do anything about it? If
and when should a company monitor its employee's e-mail?

Related Reference: Schweik, Charles M. (1995). Electronic mail, privacy and the
public sector: Guidelines for public employees and organizations. *Employee
Responsibilities and Rights Journal*, Vol.8, No.4, p.275-292.

Emotions & expressing opinions in meetings

We seem to have become the most meeting-oriented company in town. Many
of us have gone to facilitator workshops and I have seen some real benefits to
this approach. However, I've experienced some real frustration in how our
meetings have been run lately and we seem to be split as to how to handle the
problem. When anyone during the meeting feels strongly about an issue or gets a little
upset with what someone else is saying, the facilitator shuts that individual down. I feel
it's important to get things out on the table. The facilitator argues that we need to keep
our feelings out and focus on the issue. What are your thoughts?

Key Words / Concepts: facilitator, trainer, group decision making, conflict, cohesion, groupthink, problem-solving styles

Discussion Points: Should facilitators be brought in from outside the department or company to work with departmental meetings? How much conflict is appropriate at a meeting? Can there be conflict without emotion?

Related Reference: Kaeter, Margaret (1995). Facilitators: More than meeting leaders. *Training*, July, Vol.32, No.7, p60-65.

Employment-at-will

My boss called me into his office today and informed me that I needed to stop wearing perfume to work effective immediately. When I asked him if someone had complained, he said the smell was overpowering and he personally had a problem with it. I told him that I was offended, that this particular blend was extremely expensive, and without it I didn't feel dressed. I told him that I also thought it was a ridiculous request given that we have customers in our office all the time who wear colognes and perfumes of all types. Would we deny them access to our office if they offended his nose? He then told me he did not want to discuss it further and that I needed to either lose the perfume or lose my job. When I pointed out to him that my performance had been top notch and he would be terminating me without just cause, he barked back at me that he could and would fire anyone for any reason he wanted, or no reason at all. What do you say?

Key Words / Concepts: wrongful discharge, policy manuals, employee handbooks, termination, firing, implied contracts, "just cause"

Discussion Points: What are the rights of an employee and an employer in an employment relationship?

Related Reference: Dunford, Benjamin B. and Devine, Dennis J. (1998). Employment-at-will and employee discharge: a justice perspective on legal action following termination. *Personnel Psychology*, Winter, Vol.51, p.903-905.

Empowerment

I've been a supervisor here for 15 years. My company has been singing the praises of empowerment for the last three years. They want to give the workers more freedom to do what they want to do, rather than what I think they should do. While this stuff sounds pretty good, these human resource geniuses and their consultants ought to come down here and take a good look at some of these people they want to empower. The people who work for me want to be told what to do. How can I make my company realize that most of the people to whom they want to give this power don't want it and couldn't handle it anyway?

Key Words / Concepts: empowerment, total quality management, continuous improvement, self-leadership, directive leadership, participative management, self-fulfilling prophecy

Discussion Points: What actions might make this company's program more successful? What is empowerment and is it a good strategy for all organizations? Why or why not? Is empowerment desired by most employees? Why might there be some resistance to voicing an opinion or taking on more responsibility and authority?

Related Reference: Alcorn, David S. (1992). Dynamic followership: Empowerment at work. *Management Quarterly*, Spring, Vol.33, No.1, 9-13.

Expatriate manager

A multinational company has recently purchased us. The new company has asked us to select an individual to fill a job posting in a company office in Hong Kong, which will focus on our line of the business. Our new owners are providing no help, so I figure they are testing us. What procedures should we follow given that we have never done this before? Which qualities should we consider in attempting to fill this position?

Key Words / Concepts: international staffing, job analysis, adaptability screening, national culture, organizational culture, internal job candidates

Discussion Points: How does this problem differ from traditional hiring decisions? Would this situation be approached differently if (a) the job opening was in Europe or

(b) the posting did not come down from the parent organization but was internally generated?

Related Reference: Joinson, Carla (1998). Why HR managers need to think globally? *HR Magazine*, April, Vol.43, No.5, p.2-8.

F

Family concerns & questions

We are filling a job in our South American operation, headquartered in Rio de Janeiro. Our current manager there is ending his assignment two years early because his wife and family could not adjust to the country, particularly because she couldn't find work there. We don't want to make the same mistake twice, so I want to ask our candidates about how they believe their spouses and families will adjust to Brazil and its culture. When I ran this idea by our human resource director, he gave me a sour look and told me that asking questions about family members was out of bounds and illegal. It is very costly to us to bring our current manager out early. What do you think we should do?

Key Words / Concepts: expatriate assignments, national culture, adaptability screening, flexibility, family adaptability, cultural training, discrimination

Discussion Points: Assume that you are hiring internally for a management position at a company plant in a very undesirable small-town location elsewhere in the United States. You want the person you transfer to the position to stay at least five years, but you are worried that the spouses and children of your three best candidates would not want to live in this place. Do you ask these candidates about their family situations or do you get other candidates? Discuss these and other options for filling this position considering your concerns.

Related Reference: Harvey, Michael (1997). Dual-career expatriates: Expectations, adjustment and satisfaction with international relocation. *Journal of International Business Studies*, Third Quarter, Vol.28, No.3, 627-658.

Fetal protection policy

I work in a long-term care environment, with a population whose behavior is quite unpredictable and frequently violent. I am concerned about injuries in general, but specifically I am concerned about injuries to our pregnant employees and potential harm to the fetus. We recently had two employees kicked in the stomach by residents. We are considering restricting pregnant employees' work, even though no restrictions have been made by their physicians. Your thoughts?

Key Words/Concepts: sexual discrimination, fetal protection rules, violence in the workplace, employer liability, Johnson Controls, Pregnancy Discrimination Act of 1978

Discussion Points: How does the employer balance the need to protect employees from being hurt with the need to obey antidiscrimination laws? Is there a way to do both in the situation described here? Which is more important, because both might result in lawsuits against the employer?

Related Reference: Shellenberger, Sue (1998). Recent suits make pregnancy issues workplace issues. *The Wall Street Journal*, January 14, p.B1, col.1.

FMLA

I run a business with 20 employees. I'm concerned because my main assistant who does our payroll—among other things—told me she's pregnant and wants to take 12 weeks of unpaid leave after the baby is born. She says it's a federal law that I provide this leave and then give her the same job back when she returns. My employee benefits package provides for four weeks of temporary disability income for employees. I had planned to give her a month of paid leave and have a temp do the work in the meantime. I think 12 weeks is too long for her to be out of the loop. This is upsetting because she has been a valuable employee for five years. I've never been faced with this situation before because all of my other employees are men or older women. What should I do?

Key Words / Concepts: Family and Medical Leave Act, sick leave, short-term disability, Pregnancy Discrimination Act of 1978, medical certification

Discussion Points: Should companies be required by law to provide *paid* leave to employees who have recently given birth or who need to provide long-term care for a sick family member or elderly parent? Should paid leave be granted to fathers of newborn children? Should employers attempt to balance work and family life of employees or is that the responsibility of the employee?

Related Reference: Papa, Jeri White, Kopelman, Richard E. and Flynn, Gillian (1998). Sizing up the FMLA. *Workforce*, August, Vol.77, No. 8, p.38-43.

G

Gambling

At about this time every year, our office gets NCAA tournament fever in a big way. Long before the first tip-off, the office pool is formed and we all get a chance for glory and the fairly substantial pot of cash. The person who sets up the pool makes no money off the venture, the wagers are small, and it seems to bring a lot of camaraderie to the workplace. I thought everyone was enjoying the excitement of our "March Madness" pool until the self-designated pool "administrator," who's in my department, received a nasty memo from a manager in another department. The memo stated that the pool was occupying the time and energy of employees who were hired to work and not be entertained; that the pool encouraged an addictive behavior that was detrimental to both the organization and society; and that the pool should be stopped immediately. The guy then went to the boss to complain. The boss is considering the need for a new policy addressing gambling, but at least is willing to wait until after the "Final Four." A policy on prohibiting the office pool seems unduly restrictive to me and I believe it will have a negative impact on morale. When my department got wind of the memo, they were ready to go out and slash the guy's tires. Do you have any suggestions on how to deal with this situation?

Key Words / Concepts: gambling addiction, employee morale, paycheck poker, Internet gambling

Discussion Points: How valuable is the use of an office betting pool as a tool to build cohesion among employees? If an office pool is banned, might company employees turn to the Internet as an outlet for gambling on major sports events? Would it be better for the company to use the pool as an incentive to keep the employees from using company time and resources to gamble on the Internet, or to set up a policy to ban all gambling at work?

Related Reference: Ramsay, Robert D. (1995). Compulsive gambler on the payroll? *Supervision*, December, Vol.56, p.6-9.

Gender & leadership

Valerie and I were recently promoted to supervisory positions. We didn't know each other that well before, but our jobs require us to work together because our new departments must coordinate their activities closely. I don't know if it's because she's a woman and I'm a man, but we can't seem to get along. She doesn't have the drive and enthusiasm that I have, and it seems like it takes her forever to make a decision because she's always getting the employees' opinions. Can you suggest some ways we could improve our working relationship?

Key Words / Concepts: leadership style, servant leadership, intrinsic motivation, communication, power, personality, participative management

Discussion Points: Have you ever known men who, as leaders, seemed to lack drive and enthusiasm and wanted to consult with employees before making a decision? What happened? Were they successful leaders? What about women leaders who had the qualities of this male supervisor? Were they successful?

Related Reference: Koonce, Richard (1997). Language, sex, and power: Women and men in the workplace. *Training & Development*, September, Vol. 51, No.9, p.34-39.

Gossip

Our company has a real problem with office gossip and rumors reducing employee productivity and morale. Are there any training videos that you have found to be effective in addressing this issue? I'd like to put a training program together to help employees understand the destructive nature of office gossip and rumors.

Key Words / Concepts: grapevine, empowerment, employee commitment, employee participation programs

Discussion Points: Can the grapevine be eliminated or controlled through training programs or increased employee participation? Is the grapevine inevitable no matter what action management takes? If so, what, if anything, can be done regarding the spread of false rumors and gossip?

Related Reference: Danziger, Elizabeth (1988). Minimize office gossip. *Personnel Journal*, November, Vol.67, No.11, p.31-33.

Group conflict

I'm the team leader of a group of four other people. I'm happy and content with the way things are at my company and on our team, but my team members don't seem to feel that way. One member of our group just doesn't care about anything; another member is always pestering everyone to change things; another one, who's been at the company for many years, does a good job at work and is very easy going with the other members. The last member spends her time attacking everyone when we try to work together as a team. Any advice on how to get these people to work together?

Key Words / Concepts: group cohesion, team building, roles, work relationships, personality differences

Discussion Points: Are these types of people typically found on every team? Why or why not?

Related Reference: Pelled, Lisa Hope, Eisenhardt, Kathleen M., and Xin, Katherine R. (1999). Exploring the black box: an analysis of work group diversity, conflict, and performance. *Administrative Science Quarterly*, March, Vol.44, p.1-28.

Health inquiries of job applicants

Does the Americans with Disabilities Act prohibit me from asking about the health of job applicants? Could my company get in trouble if we give physical exams to those who have disabilities?

Key Words / Concepts: employee health, Americans with Disabilities Act, alcoholism and substance abuse, smoking, job descriptions, physical examinations

Discussion Points: Why would an organization want or need to know the health of a job applicant?

Related Reference: Palmer, Keith (1995). How can you be sure your employees are fit for work? *People Management*, May 18, Vol.1, No.10, p.51.

Health plan alternatives

Our organization now offers several alternatives to the traditional 80/20 insurance plan. Recently we've been having difficulty with one of the HMO plans. Our people have complained about delays in getting referrals to specialists, and in the case of one employee, the HMO would not pay for a set of tests that would have saved her a lot of worry. She ended up paying for them out of her own pocket. All this is quite different from our other two HMOs, but you'd never be able to tell it from the HMO literature or their presentations. How can we give our employees better choices in the future, and is there anything that can be done about our existing problem?

Key Words / Concepts: health benefit costs, health insurance, flexible benefits program, cafeteria plan

Discussion Points: Research recent articles about HMOs and PPOs and legislative efforts to regulate them. What legal restrictions, if any, should be placed on HMOs? To what extent should a human resource manager be involved in ensuring that plans used by the company follow practices that you consider to be legal and ethical? How can a human resource manager find information about HMO and PPO performance?

Related Reference: Kalish, Bradley (1998). PPOs deliver what HMOs don't. *Modern Healthcare*, April 20, Vol.28, No.16, p.96.

Height & weight inquiries of applicants

My 17-year-old daughter just completed an application at a well-known national clothing store and was invited to an interview a week later. When she arrived for the interview, she was given a piece of paper with a couple of questions on it that surprised both of us. Two questions asked what her height and weight were. I didn't think those types of questions could be asked. Can they?

Key Words / Concepts: BFOQ, business necessity, discrimination

Discussion Points: Could the company have a legitimate need to have the information requested? Why or why not? Could it find the information relevant to job performance by other means than asking these questions? How?

Related Reference: McEvoy, Sharlene A. (1992). Fat chance: Employment discrimination against the overweight. *Labor Law Journal*, January, Vol.43, No.1, p.3-14.

Honesty tests

I run a chain of seven farm implement stores in small Mississippi towns. My employee turnover in these stores is relatively low, but it's pretty clear that some of the employees—new hires as well as those who have been with the business for a long time—are taking merchandise home or letting their friends and relatives steal us blind. I have had to fire three employees within the last six months and I may fire several more in the next three. I understand that lie detector tests for job applicants may be questionable, but I need some way to test the honesty of my people before I hire them. Any suggestions?

Key Words / Concepts: criterion validity, content validity, reliability, Employee Polygraph Protection Act, employee theft

Discussion Points: Is use of a lie detector in this case appropriate? Why or why not? How should honesty be tested in this situation? Should applicants for jobs be tested as well as current employees?

Related Reference: Smith, Greg (1997). What you need to know about pre-employment tests. *Career World*, September, Vol.26, No.1, p.22-25.

Hygiene

We've got a rather foul problem with a fellow supervisor at our office.
Jack is a fine employee and manager who gets along well with the rest of us and seems to do OK with the customers who visit the company. We hate to raise a stink, but that's the problem. It's apparent that Jack does not bathe or use deodorant on a regular basis and can be very unpleasant to be near, particularly for any length of time. We have discussed putting soap or deodorant on his desk anonymously or even giving it to him as a Christmas present. If we're noticing this smell, the customers must be too. Maybe this is a cultural thing because Jack came here from another country not too long ago. Do you have any suggestions for dealing with this problem?

Key Words / Concepts: hygiene, Americans with Disabilities Act, national culture, guaranteed fair treatment, employee discipline

Discussion Points: Identify aspects of other countries' cultures that might clash with elements of U.S. culture or regional elements of U.S. culture that could clash, creating problems in the workplace. What approach should the human resource manager take if confronted with the problem described in this question?

Related Reference: Hirschman, Carolyn (1998). Who's going to tell her? *HR Magazine*, February, Vol.43, No.2, p.102-108.

I

Incentives

 I work at a small gift shop with six other women; three of us work full time and the four others are part-timers. A couple of months ago, the two owners decided to start an incentive program. Each of us was assigned a section of the store to stock and keep looking nice, and we would vote at the end of the month as to who did the best job. The winner would get a $50 bonus. At the end of the month, there was a vote (even the owners and manager voted!) and two of the part-timers were tied so they both got $50. I don't feel this was fair because the four part-timers did not do their share of answering the telephone and waiting on customers; instead they spent all of their time sprucing up their sections. We are upset because this incentive system did not reward the full-timers. We work harder than the others who are only there two or three days a week. How could the owners have designed a better incentive program?

Key Words / Concepts: bonus, merit pay plan, employee participation, piecework plan, equity and fairness

Discussion Points: Are bonuses a better incentive than raises? Should the rank-and-file employees decide on the amount of the bonus or should that be left up to management? How does the company encourage an employee to look out for the good of the entire business and not just the part where the particular employee works?

Related Reference: Robbins, C. B. (1983). Design effective incentive plans. *Personnel Administrator*, Vol.28, No.5, p.8-10.

Independent contractors

 I understand that if I classify my employees as independent contractors rather than employees, I can save a great deal of money and paperwork. How do I go about doing this?

Key Words / Concepts: control systems, outsourcing, job descriptions, wage and hour laws, Internal Revenue Service, position analysis questionnaire

Discussion Points: How closely does an employer need to monitor the work force? How would this system work if the employer is (a) a small manufacturer, (b) a bicycle messenger service, or (c) a seller of resort properties and condominiums?

Related Reference: Cronin, Michael P. (1994). Does this look like an employee to you? *Inc.*, September, Vol.16, No.9, p. 50.

Internet use/abuse

Recently, we linked up with the Internet at our company, believing that its research capabilities would help us in our business. We also established a web page for people to learn more about our organization. After a few weeks, I saw several of my employees connecting to the net to review the latest sports scores and the latest entertainment gossip. These activities occurred during business hours when these people should have been working.

I'm afraid many other employees also are abusing the Internet link. They may be "surfing" the World Wide Web's want ads for new jobs or downloading pornography. What should I do?

Key Words/Concepts: Internet, Intranet, World Wide Web, hostile work environment, employment planning, recruiting, organizational strategy and HR policies, employee privacy

Discussion Points: Identify the potential pros and cons of establishing Internet connections for employees and managers. Is the Internet a positive or negative force for the workplace? Why? Should employees be allowed to "surf" at will?

Related Reference: Oravec, Jo Anne (1999). Working hard and playing hard: Constructive uses of on-line recreation. *Journal of General Management*, Spring, Vol.24, p.77-88.

Interview questions & sex discrimination

? I operate a telemarketing firm and I'm concerned about whether my female employees will be able to work long hours, nights, and weekends without it creating problems with their husbands and children. How should I ask job applicants about this during the hiring process?

Key Words / Concepts: equal opportunity, Title VII, sex discrimination, disparate treatment, disparate impact, marital status

Discussion Points: What should an interviewer say if a job applicant raises the concern mentioned in the question about night and weekend hours taking away from time with the family? What other issues might an interviewer want to ask about that could be considered potentially discriminatory?

Related Reference: McShulskis, Elaine (1997). Small businesses: Be aware of illegal interview questions. *HRMagazine*, June, Vol.42, No.6, p.22.

J

Job descriptions

? We're in the annual, time-consuming, mind-numbing process of reviewing and updating job descriptions in our company. Since we've moved to teams and now have projects that come and go, the lines that defined the jobs have become a lot fuzzier. I've heard most companies in the same boat have eliminated job descriptions altogether because the work that is done changes virtually every day. It sure makes sense to me, given that I last looked at the job descriptions in our department when I was reviewing and updating them a year ago at this time. Do you have any examples of companies that successfully trashed their job descriptions?

Key Words / Concepts: job analysis, job descriptions, de-jobbing, job evaluation

Discussion Points: Do you have a job description? If so, to what extent is the actual work you perform reflected in the job description? What are the advantages of job descriptions? Disadvantages?

Related Reference: Halcrow, Allan (1999). Reality doesn't have a job description. *Workforce*, Dec., Vol.78, No.12, p.12.

Job hopping

I've been reviewing resumes for a managerial position in our organization. Surprisingly, most of the applicants have had what I would term a "checkered" past. More than half of the applicants held positions in four or more organizations in a 10-year period. Although all of these moves appeared to be voluntary on their part, I think a minimum amount of time an employee should remain with a company before moving on is four years. I view these frequent job-hoppers as a bad risk. I feel that their frequent job changes demonstrate a lack personal stability, unrealistic expectations, and a lack of commitment to their past employer that will soon become a lack of commitment to my company if I hire them.

In passing, I griped about the lousy pool of applicants to a friend of mine, and he said that I was way off base. He asked me if I'd rather have an outstanding employee who came in for a short period of time and made significant contributions or a 10-year employee whose contributions were minimal. He argued that loyalty doesn't count for anything anymore and if you don't switch companies every couple of years, people think there's something wrong with you because you're not moving fast enough. Who's right?

Key Words / Concepts: career change, turnover, job change, loyalty, organizational commitment, supply and demand

Discussion Points: What problems occur when turnover in an organization is high? How might you determine whether your organization's turnover rate is too high? What strategies could an organization employ to reduce job hopping?

Related Reference: Half, Robert (1996). How many job hops can I get away with? *Management Accounting*, July, Vol.78, No.1, p.12.

Jokes & humor at work

Let me premise my question by stating up front that I like a good laugh as much as the next guy. But my employees seem to be making me and the way I run the company the target of jokes and jabs a bit more frequently than I feel is appropriate. It started innocently enough. First, a few "Dilbert" cartoons started to float around the office. Then my employees started putting cartoons on the walls of their cubicles or on their office doors. They have "Dilbert" calendars on their desks, and I noticed that one employee even has a "Dilbert Voodoo Boss" on top of her computer monitor. I became really upset this morning when I found a cartoon taped in our break room with the note scrawled across the bottom: "Can you relate?" Am I just being paranoid or should I ban these postings from the office with the justification of maintaining a professional atmosphere?

DILBERT reprinted by permission of United Feature Syndicate, Inc.

Key Words / Concepts: humor, attitudes, job satisfaction, ethnic jokes

Discussion Points: How far is "too far" when it comes to jokes in the workplace? Can the appropriate use of humor benefit the organization? Under what circumstances?

Related Reference: Avolio, B., Howell, J., & Sosik, J. (1999). A funny thing happened on the way to the bottom line: Humor as a moderator of leadership style effects. *Academy of Management Journal*, Vol. 42, No.2, p.219-227.

K

Key job responsibilities

 To say that the right hand doesn't know what the left hand is doing is putting it mildly when it comes to my office. There were three decisions made this week in which I should have been involved and with which I will now have to live for the next year. The previous week another department manager sent one of his employees to call on a prospect that I had already developed. We looked like idiots. Any suggestions to keep this from occurring down the road?

Key Words / Concepts: key responsibility charting, group decision making, job analysis, job description, job enrichment

Discussion Points: What are the positive points of group decision making? What are its negative points? What kinds of decisions are better left up to individuals and which ones should be the responsibility of the group? Should a human resource manager encourage line managers to involve employees in the decision-making process? When so many activities in an organization must be coordinated, how can the HR manager assist with the process?

Related Reference: Carr, Clay (1994). Empowered organizations, empowering leaders. *Training & Development*, March, Vol.48, No.3, p.39-44.

Kidnapping, terrorism, & security while abroad

We're about to send two of our managers on a fact-finding trip to several South American countries to develop new business opportunities. One of our managers read an article about terrorists kidnapping business travelers in Central and South America. Should we be concerned? How can we make security arrangements? What are the most dangerous countries for our managers to be in?

Key Words / Concepts: violence at work, security measures, management training, expatriate managers, unsafe conditions, employment planning, terrorism

Discussion Points: Identify and rank the activities that present the greatest health and safety risks for managers who are assigned overseas. Does kidnapping on an overseas assignment appear to be a serious threat? Does the risk of terrorism indicate that business activities be curtailed in certain countries? Under what hazardous circumstances should expatriate managers be withdrawn from job assignments? How should companies prepare for this eventuality?

Related Reference: Greengard, Samuel (1997). Mission possible: Protecting employees abroad. *Workforce*, August, Vol.76, No.3, p.30-36.

L

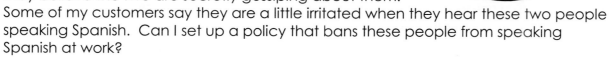

Language restrictions

? I recently hired two Hispanic employees who sometimes speak in Spanish to each other at the office. This is starting to cause problems because some of my other workers are complaining that they believe the two are secretly gossiping about them. Some of my customers say they are a little irritated when they hear these two people speaking Spanish. Can I set up a policy that bans these people from speaking Spanish at work?

Key Words / Concepts: Title VII, company policy, cultural awareness, cross-cultural training, language training, diversity

Discussion Points: If and when would the restrictions suggested in the question be proper and legal? How would a policy imposing language restrictions on employees be worded? What problems could such a policy cause?

Related Reference: Fink, Ross L., Robinson, Robert K. & Wyld, David C. (1996). English-only work rules: Balancing fair employment considerations in a multicultural and multilingual healthcare workforce. *Hospital & Health Services Administration*, Winter, Vol.41, No.4, p.473-483.

Leadership style

? I've been a manager for 15 years, and I've always run a tight ship in my department. The employees do what I tell them to do, and, if they don't, they walk. Because of this, they know what to expect, and things run smoothly— that is, until top management imposed this "participative management" baloney in our company. Why should I be forced to change my leadership style so that people who have nothing of value to contribute can "participate"?

Key Words / Concepts: team building; managerial grid; directive, participative, and laissez-faire styles of leadership; organizational development; management development

Discussion Points: Under what circumstances would the leadership style suggested by the question be appropriate? What kinds of development programs are needed to address the issues in this question?

Related Reference: Peterson, Randall S. (1997). A directive leadership style in group decision making can be both virtue and vice: Evidence from elite and experimental groups. *Journal of Personality & Social Psychology*, Vol.72, p.1107-1121.

Learning organization

? My boss does a great job of talking one thing and doing something else. He constantly tells us he wants our company to be a learning organization, but whenever we try to do something innovative, he jumps on us because either our actions are too out of the ordinary or because we mess up in some regard. It is difficult for middle managers such as me to know what he really wants, but we do think it is a good idea to be innovative. Do you have any suggestions on how we can become a learning organization despite the negative feedback we get from the boss?

Key Words / Concepts: behavior modeling, espoused theory, theory-in-use, systems thinking, shared vision

Discussion Points: What kind of organizational culture exists in this company? How can the human resources department help an organization to be innovative?

Related Reference: Tichy, Noel M. & Cohen, Eli (1998). The teaching organization. *Training & Development*, Vol.52, No.7, p.26-33.

M

Micro-management

? I've been with my company for nine years and over this period of time have had three wonderful bosses. Each one gave me the freedom to do my job the way I saw fit and, in turn, I was able to empower my employees to use their skills and abilities to the fullest. Our division has always been known for its innovative products, high levels of productivity, and the ability to quickly solve problems. I believe this success was largely due to the leadership style of these three bosses. The problem now is our new boss. We can't make a single decision without clearing it with him first. Every decision I've made in the past six months has been either second guessed or overturned by him. In addition, if any of the division heads disagree with him on any issue, they are labeled as "not being a team player." He argues that tight controls and his involvement in every decision are critical because he has the ultimate responsibility to get the job done and get it done correctly. Lastly, the company's surge in customer complaints and decline in employee morale since he took over is being attributed to our inability to control our people. How can I work effectively with this guy?

Key Words / Concepts: autonomy, control, morale, delegation, leadership style

Discussion Points: What is the role of the human resource manager in mediating this relationship? Why does micro-management occur? What are its consequences?

Related Reference: Kerfoot, K. (1998). Micro-managing or leading: The clinician's challenge. *Nursing Economics*, Sept.-Oct., Vol.16, No.5, p.282-283.

Military leave

I have an employee who was hired last month to perform a weekend-only part-time job for me. Out of the blue he has told his supervisor that he is in the National Guard and must serve one weekend per month in addition to the traditional two weeks during the summer. He never shared his National Guard commitment with the interviewer or supervisor during the hiring process. Are there any legal ramifications for the company if we let him go because he can't work the schedule for which we hired him?

Key Words / Concepts: reservists, National Guard duty, leave time, HR planning, discrimination

Discussion Points: How can employers prepare for and deal with staffing issues that occur if reservists and National Guard members are sent away on extended assignments?

Related Reference: Evans, Barbara Ryniker (1997) Understanding military leave laws. *Supervision*, November, Vol.58, No.11, p.14-16.

Money as a motivator

Recently I read a newspaper article about a survey that found that money no longer motivates employees. The survey said companies should stress improving the quality of work, more open communication, and more concern for an employee's family life rather than increasing wages and benefits. My employees still seem to want more money. What's their problem?

Key Words / Concepts: hierarchy of needs, motivator-hygiene theory, expectancy theory, pay-for-performance plans, quality-improvement teams, piecework

Discussion Points: Evaluate the different factors that motivate employees to provide effort on the job. Does money serve as a personal source of motivation to you in your job? How does money rank among the various rewards you might receive for doing your job?

Related Reference: Kohn, Alfie (1998). Challenging Behavioralist Dogma: Myths about money and motivation. *Compensation and Benefits Review*, March-April, p.27, 33-37.

N

Napping at work

I received a complaint from a production employee last week who said that his foreman was upset with him because he took 10-minute naps on his break in the break room. He has never overslept and has a wristwatch alarm clock to prevent this from happening. Apparently the foreman has had problems with others in the past who have taken extended naps (two hours or more), so he has forbidden naps entirely. Does a person have the right to do what they wish during their breaks? There is no written policy that specifically prohibits this. The employee claims he's usually not even napping. He just needs to close his eyes periodically because of the irritants in the shop's air.

Key Words / Concepts: workers' compensation, OSHA, break time, paid time-off

Discussion Points: If napping is acceptable on breaks, are there any employee behaviors that might be unacceptable on break times?

Related Reference: Paul, A. M. (1998). Sleeping on the job. *Psychology Today*, Nov.-Dec., Vol.31, No.6, p.14.

Natural attrition

Over the last few years, our organization has been shrinking through natural attrition. As employees leave, they're not replaced, and we attempt to pick up the slack. Although this strategy has increased our profit margins, we've alienated a lot of our customers, who expect the level of quality we had offered before the staff cutbacks. In addition, I lost one of my best employees yesterday who was fed up with the excessive work load and no end in sight. Our CEO doesn't feel there is a problem because overall organizational profits are up. He argued that all organizations must do more with less and if someone's not happy, then it's best that he or she leave. I feel as if I'm on a sinking ship. Am I missing something?

Key Words / Concepts: financial objectives, social objectives, measurement of work, short-term/long-term trade-offs, long-range goals

Discussion Points: What are some measures other than profits, costs, and productivity that can be used to measure effectiveness in an organization? How can a human resource manager assist the top management in establishing those measures?

Related Reference: Hequet, Marc (1995). Doing more with less. *Training*, October, Vol.32, No.10, p.77-80.

Nosy boss

"Fred," who is a long-time supervisor at my company, is constantly discussing our employees' personal difficulties with them. For example, they have talked about fights they are having with their spouses, an unwanted pregnancy, and similar problems—even alcohol abuse. Some of the employees think he is a good boss because they can talk to him (and he doesn't require much work out of them), but others have complained that he gossips to others about these problems. He doesn't seem as interested about work as much as he is in being the first to know about some personal scuttlebutt. What should I do?

Key Words / Concepts: employee assistance program (EAP), confidentiality, job-related information, trust violation, grapevine, need for affiliation

Discussion Points: How much should supervisors know about their employees' personal lives? To what extent, if any, should they intervene to assist employees in dealing with personal problems? What should the position of the human resource manager be in regard to such interventions by line managers?

Related Reference: McCune, Jenny C. (1998). The elusive thing called trust. *Management Review*, July-August, Vol.87, No.7, p.10-16.

O

Off-duty conduct

 I am fortunate to have a fantastic group of employees who work for me. However, one gentleman in particular is spectacular. He has a tremendous work ethic, is always a top producer, and has been "employee of the month" as many times as it's possible to be nominated within a year's period. My problems and his occurred after I bragged on his performance to my boss. During our conversation, I commented that it was hard to believe how great a job this guy was doing while holding down a second job in his spare time. With that comment, the boss came unglued and made it clear that either the employee was to quit the second job or I'd have to terminate him. It's not like this guy is selling trade secrets. His second job has nothing to do with our business, and he really seems to need the extra cash. Further, I can't imagine that forcing him to quit the second job is even legal, because it's on his own time. My thinking is that if I'm unable to change my boss's mind, it's very likely my employee will quit or, at best, his morale will be shot to hell. How can I convince my boss other than again pointing out that he's a spectacular employee and bringing up possible legal problems?

Key Words / Concepts: moonlighting, employment-at-will, employee privacy, organizational commitment, job performance

Discussion Points: In what circumstances is working a part-time job elsewhere inappropriate for an employee? If necessary, what can employers do to discourage their employees from moonlighting but not discourage their morale?

Related Reference: Dworkin, Morehead (1997). It's my life--leave me alone: off-the-job employee associated privacy rights. *American Business Law Journal*, Fall, Vol.35, No. 1, p.47-103.

Older workers

We are filling a sales management position that requires a great deal of traveling to develop new business, and we would like to promote from within. My problem is we have several good internal candidates for the position, all of whom have been inside supervisors at our local offices. One of these applicants is a 57-year-old employee who has six years as a supervisor and has been with the company for 10 years after he was "downsized" by a competitor. His experience seems to fit the job better than that of the other applicants, but I am concerned that his energy level and health will not suit the long hours, frequent travel, and many sales meetings the job will entail. We have other candidates who can handle the travel, but they'll need additional training. I know that legally I probably shouldn't be bringing up age. However, it sure seems relevant in this case. What should I do?

Key Words / Concepts: career planning and development, career stages, maintenance stage, decline stage, occupational skills, age discrimination, stereotyping

Discussion Points: Evaluate the selection process at this company based on the information included in the question. How might the process be improved? What kinds of images might employers have of college students who apply for jobs with their companies? Why might these employers have such ideas?

Related Reference: Lefkoveck, J. L. (1992). Older workers: Why and how to capitalize on their powers. *Employment Relations Today*, Vol.19, No.1, p.63-79.

OSHA audits

I run a company that has about 200 employees. We are a light manufacturer that uses some hazardous materials. I'm concerned for two reasons. First, we had a serious accident last week when one of the employees fell down some steps and broke his leg. Second, a friend of mine who also owns a business had an accident at his company six months ago, and five employees were hurt. The accident was followed by an OSHA inspection, and he had to pay several thousand dollars in fines. What can I do to make sure I can avoid such fines if my company gets inspected because of this accident?

Key Words / Concepts: Occupational Safety and Health Act, Occupational Safety and Health Administration, OSHA standards, citations, unsafe conditions, unsafe acts, workers' compensation

Discussion Points: Contrast the legal responsibilities of the employer to provide a safe workplace with the employer's ethical responsibilities to ensure that employees are not injured on the job. How does OSHA relate to an employer's legal and ethical responsibilities? Is smoking in the workplace a matter of employee health and safety subject to government regulation? Explain.

Related Reference: Thompson, Neville (1993). Conduct constructive safety audits. *HRMagazine*, July, Vol.38, No.7, p.55-56.

Overtime

 Our company is paying too much overtime to hourly employees. My partner suggests moving away from hourly employees and creating an all-salaried workforce to eliminate the overtime. What are the pitfalls of this plan?

Key Words / Concepts: Fair Labor Standards Act, exempt employees, all-salaried workforce, nonexempt employees, fluctuating workweek formula

Discussion Points: What might be the impact on workforce performance if overtime is eliminated? What might be better strategies for trimming overtime costs than the one mentioned here? What is the true definition of exempt employees and how does that relate to this question?

Related Reference: Martin, Christopher L. & Newman, Jerry M. (1992). The FLSA overtime provision: A new controversy?, *Compensation and Benefits Review*, July-August, Vol. 24, No.4., 60-63.

P

Pay secrecy

In a recent memo, my company restated its position that "no employee should discuss his or her level of compensation with any other employee." Regardless of what management says, people are going to talk and I hate to lose a good employee over this rigid policy. Haven't these secret pay plans been found to hurt rather than help companies anyway? How much and what kinds of information regarding pay should take place?

Key Words / Concepts: job evaluation, pay plans, equity, distributive justice, procedural justice, communication

Discussion Points: What are the reasons why a company would have a policy against its employees sharing their compensation levels with other employees? What are the arguments against instituting such policies? Do some companies shy away from open pay policies because they do not want employees to know how much the managers are paid? Why or why not?

Related Reference: Bartol, K. M. & Martin, D. C. (1988). Influences on managerial pay allocations: A dependency perspective. *Personnel Psychology*, Vol.41, p.361-378.

Performance evaluation & the angry employee

I've been in management a little over a year and just got my first taste of performance evaluation from the other side of the table. It was a disaster! I made some very specific comments about substandard work and how it could be improved. All I got was anger, defensiveness, and the feeling that I did a lot more harm than good. I spoke with several other managers, some with five years of management experience in our company, who also dread these feedback sessions. They claimed to have gotten similar reactions from their employees when they give anything but glowing comments. Do we have a tough bunch of employees to deal with or are we doing something wrong? I cannot imagine ever showing any anger toward my boss because of his evaluation of my performance. What's with these people!?

Key Words / Concepts: defensive behavior, stress, burnout, workplace violence, continual feedback

Discussion Points: What is the best way for a supervisor to prepare for a feedback session with an employee? What kind of guidance can the human resource manager provide to supervisors on how to conduct these sessions? Why might the employees at this company react this way to criticism?

Related Reference: Korsgaard, M. Audrey & Roberson, Loriann (1995). Procedural justice in performance evaluation: The role of instrumental and non-instrumental voice in performance appraisal discussions. *Journal of Management*, Vol.21, No.4, p.657-669.

Performance feedback & career

development

I'm the personnel manager at a small company of about 100 employees. My boss, the CEO, wants me to develop a performance feedback system that will help develop the employees. The idea is to use these sessions strictly for employee growth. Pay increases would not be directly affected by the performance feedback. The CEO is going to continue to decide the pay raises apart from these sessions.

The problem is this: There is one supervisor here who should not be involved in the feedback process because she has absolutely no tact and the employees working under her would gain nothing from it. She seems to know her employees better than anyone, however, so it would be hard to do this program without her. Any suggestions?

Key Words / Concepts: management development, interpersonal skills, supervisory skills, reinforcement process, succession planning, developmental performance appraisal

Discussion Points: How can a management development program be incorporated into the performance appraisal process? Should developmental performance appraisals such as those discussed here be tied to pay increases? Why or why not?

Related Reference: Arvey, R.D. & Murphy, K.R. (1998). Performance evaluation in work settings. *Annual Review of Psychology*, Vol.49, p.141-168.

Personality conflicts

My co-workers are fun to work with, except for Mary Ellen, who always seems to be scheming to make herself look good at our expense. She is always playing little games, buttering herself up in front of the office manager, and lying to and about everyone for any influence she can possibly get. She has just been promoted to supervisor because of her ability to lie and manipulate her co-workers and the managers here. We all hate her. What can we do?

Key Words / Concepts: personality testing, "Big Five" personality dimensions, projective personality tests, Machiavellianism, test validity

Discussion Points: Evaluate the relative importance of knowledge, skills, abilities, and personality traits in making a hiring decision. Would this answer need to be adjusted based upon whether the company is hiring a manager or an hourly employee? How?

Related Reference: Mook, Jonathan R. (1996). Personality testing in today's workplace: Avoiding the legal pitfalls. *Employee Relations Law Journal*, Winter, Vol.22, No.3, p.65-88.

Pregnant employees

I'm facing a big problem in my little office because two of my most talented employees have recently become pregnant—three months apart. They both want to cut back their hours to part time once their maternity leaves have been completed next spring. I don't think I can afford to do this because I need to have at least four people here 40 hours a week. I hate to lose these people because they are good employees, but I'm also concerned about whether they will sue me if I lay them off. What do you suggest?

Key Words / Concepts: Pregnancy Discrimination Act of 1978, alternative work arrangements, flextime, job sharing, telecommuting, labor market demographics

Discussion Points: How could this situation have been remedied in the employment planning process? In what instances does employee turnover have positive results for the employer? How can the employer avoid pregnancy discrimination in this case?

Related Reference: Oakes Wren, A. L., Kidwell, R. E. & Kidwell, L. A. (1996). Managing pregnancy in the workplace. *Business Horizons*, November/December, Vol.39, No.6, p.61-67.

Privacy & HRIS

Our company database system, which all employees can access, lists every employee's home phone and address. I raised this as a concern with our MIS director and he argued that such information is not considered confidential. I feel that allowing all employees access violates my rights of privacy. I don't want my unpublished number published! Am I being unreasonable?

Key Words / Concepts: Federal Privacy Act, human resource information system, information levels, confidential versus nonconfidential information, information access

Discussion Points: What legitimate reasons would a company have not to keep unpublished home phone numbers of employees confidential from other employees? What other types of information about employees might be considered confidential and not released to all employees? Should Social Security numbers of employees be kept confidential? Why or why not?

Related Reference: Harris, Donald (1987). A matter of privacy: Managing personnel data in computers. *Personnel*, February, p.34-39.

Promotion from within

 My boss just went outside the company to hire for a senior management position, passing up four of us who have been here a long time. We have been promoted from inside the company in the past, but it hasn't happened in years. We are getting demoralized. Shouldn't it be standard procedure to reward loyal employees by promoting from within?

Key Words / Concepts: succession planning, internal candidates, internal labor markets, career-oriented appraisals, job postings, managerial track, professional track

Discussion Points: What organizational factors would have an impact on the ability to promote from within? What environmental factors would have an impact on an organization's policy to promote from within? What should an employee or manager do to ensure being considered for promotion? Should promotion to management be the only way to advance in the company?

Related Reference: Bedeian, Arthur G. & Armenakis, Achilles A. (1998). The cesspool syndrome: How dreck floats to the top of declining organizations. *The Academy of Management Executive*, February, Vol.12, No.1, p.58-67.

Promotion to management

After six years working on the clerical staff, I've just been promoted to office manager. I'm concerned about making the change to my new job next month because I'm afraid my old friends and co-workers will take advantage of me. How do I gain the respect I deserve now that I'm a manager?

Key Words / Concepts: interpersonal skills, expert power, referent power, authority, seniority, competence, occupational skills, aptitudes

Discussion Points: On what basis should employers decide to promote employees into management positions? How could procedures to promote employees be designed to have positive effects on employee job satisfaction, commitment, and performance?

Related Reference: Warshaw, Michael (1998). The good guy's guide to office politics. *Fast Company*, Vol.14, p.156-178.

Quality management during a downsizing

I've had TQM in place for about two years. Although the program has increased quality and productivity and kept my company afloat, we've had a recent unexpected downturn in business. I have no choice but to lay off employees. Will these layoffs undo the progress of my quality program and make the remaining employees feel they are not valued?

Key Words / Concepts: total quality management, continuous improvement, downsizing, restructuring, empowerment, communication, trust

Discussion Points: Can downsizing occur at the same time as a quality program? Are the objectives of quality management and restructuring consistent? Why or why not?

Related Reference: Martin, Christopher L., Parsons, Charles K. & Bennett, Nathan (1995). The influence of employee involvement program membership during downsizing: Attitudes toward the employer and the union. *Journal of Management*, Vol. 21, No.5, p.879-890.

R

Reference checks

I often get called by personnel people who are doing reference checks on my former employees. I understand that companies have been sued for giving out negative information about former employees even if it's true. I also heard that if you fail to provide negative information about an employee to a company, that company can sue you for negligence. This sounds like a no-win situation. Should I refuse to talk to people who ask for reference checks?

Key Words / Concepts: employment information disclosure laws, background investigations, defamation of character

Discussion Points: How effective are reference checks in predicting an applicant's subsequent job performance? Should employers check the references listed by the applicant? Why or why not? Should employers contact people who know the applicant but are not listed as references on the employee's application? Why or why not?

Related Reference: Arnesen, David W., Fleenor, Patrick C., & Blizinsky, Marlin (1998).Name, rank and serial number? The dilemma of reference checks. *Business Horizons*, July-August, Vol.41, No.4, p.71-78.

Religion & Muzak® in the office

My boss is a very religious man and operates a mid-sized construction company. Every day, he plays gospel music over the Muzak system, coupled with the sermons of evangelist preachers. We even have a moment of silence at the start of each work day. During the holidays, he constantly plays Christmas music. I'm sick of this bombardment of religion. Isn't he violating my civil rights?

Key Words / Concepts: religious discrimination, Title VII, organizational culture, person–organization fit, realistic job preview, employer rights

Discussion Points: Is this an example of religious discrimination? Should the boss continue to play the music each day? Should the company moment of silence and music choices be made clear to employees during the selection process? Why or why not?

Related Reference: Schopf, John (1997). Religious activity and proselytization in the workplace: The murky line between healthy expression and unlawful harassment. *Columbia Journal of Law & Social Problems*, Vol.31, No.1, p.39-59.

Religious holidays & accommodation

I'm open on Christmas and I'm open on Easter. I'm up-front with new hires as to my hours and days of operation. When the holidays roll around, everybody gripes as expected. However, when I was scheduling in December this time, I had two employees flat out refuse to work on the 24th or 25th. When I told them if they didn't come in as scheduled, they could find employment elsewhere, they threatened to sue me for religious discrimination. I couldn't get a straight answer from anybody on whether or not they had a leg to stand on, and as it turned out, I was able to put together a full crew for the holiday shifts without them, so I backed down. How far must I go in making religious accommodation for my employees in terms of time off?

Key Words / Concepts: religious discrimination, accommodation, paid leave

Discussion Points: What is "reasonable" when accommodating religious beliefs? What if someone wants to wear a turban or a veil to the office? Pray at work? What if everyone wants off on Christmas eve?

Related Reference: Flynn, Gillian (1998). Accommodating religion on the job: Few rules, lots of common sense. *Workforce*, September, Vol.77, No.9 p.94-96.

Repatriation

Constance has been manager of our European operation, based in Brussels, for the last three years. She is ready to return to our headquarters office for a new assignment, actually a promotion for her and a substantial raise. Unfortunately, the office grapevine is sour with talk that she should not have received this promotion because other "deserving" managers at the headquarters were in line and were passed over. We're concerned that they will not work well with her. Several employees are already joking about how she is returning from her "European vacation." These people have no idea how hard she worked, how difficult this assignment was, and how deserving of the promotion she is. What suggestions can you make for how we should deal with the challenge of fitting her back into the headquarters operation?

Key Words / Concepts: repatriation agreements, company sponsor, reorientation programs, career counseling, communication

Discussion Points: During the time Constance was in her overseas assignment, what are some ways that company officials could have made clear to the home office employees how she was progressing—without violating her privacy?

Related Reference: Boles, Margaret (1997). How organized is your expatriate program? *Workforce*, August, Vol.76, No.8, p..21-22.

Romance in the workplace

Two of my most talented managers have been dating for about a year and recently announced that they are getting married. We don't have a policy about this, but I feel when the marriage happens, it will cause problems at work for everyone. What action can we take?

Key Words / Concepts: sexual harassment, privacy, nepotism, dual-career couples

Discussion Points: When is romance in the workplace considered sexual harassment? If a company requires people to work long hours, which limits their ability to have a social life, isn't it reasonable to expect that they might date co-workers?

Related Reference: Ceniceros, Roberto (1998). Some employers using contracts to cut romance risks. *Business Insurance*, Oct. 12, Vol.32, No.41, p.3-4

S

"Salting"

I own a small company with about 50 employees. I want to keep the company nonunion so I try to treat my people very well. I heard something recently called salting, unions sending in their members to apply for jobs in nonunion shops like mine to try and get enough workers to get the company to go union. Is this sort of deception legal? What can I do about it?

Key Words / Concepts: union shop, grievance, National Labor Relations Board, bargaining unit, authorization cards, right-to-work laws

Discussion Points: What are the legal and ethical implications of the union practice of salting, sending in union members to obtain jobs under false pretenses so they can attempt to start an organizing effort within the company? What rights does the employer have in this sort of situation?

Related Reference: Lucas, Michael D.(1997). Salting and other union tactics: A unionist's perspective. *Journal of Labor Research*, Vol.18, p.55-65.

Sexual harassment

I'm the owner of a small business and I held a company New Year's Eve party at my house this year for a few employees and clients. At the party, one of my managers wore a tie that had a picture of a naked woman on the back of it. For laughs, he kept flashing the picture to everyone, including several female employees. Could this be considered sexual harassment, even though the party was at my house and not at the office?

Key Words / Concepts: Title VII, hostile work environment, policy statements

Discussion Points: If the party had been held at an employee's—rather than the owner's—house, could the company be held liable for sexual harassment if attendees believed the tie to be offensive? Why or why not?   Under what circumstances should offsite activities be specifically covered in a company's sexual harassment policy?

Related Reference: Kirshenberg, Seth (1997). Sexual harassment: What you need to know. *Training & Development*, September, Vol.51, No.9, p.54-55.

Sick leave banks

? It has been brought to my attention that one of my employees has a terminally ill wife. He would like to spend more time with her but has used up all of his paid leave and sick leave. He has been offered an unpaid leave of absence but is financially unable to take it. A friend of mine suggested that some of the other employees may want to donate some of their days off, but I'm afraid this might open up a big can of worms. Any suggestions from you?

Key Words / Concepts: sick leave, long-term disability, short-term disability, employee benefits, cafeteria plan

Discussion Points: What problems might be caused by the donation of other employees' sick leave time? How would you deal with these problems?

Related Reference: Cowans, Deborah Shalowitz (1995). Sick leave pool. *Business Insurance*, March 13, Vol.29, No.11, p.6.

"Slackers" & withholding effort on a team

? Our restaurant wants to give our wait staff more responsibility in sharing tables, making decisions, and managing our own work without a floor supervisor telling us what to do. I'm worried because Bill is on our team, and from past experience on group tasks, my co-workers and I can see he's a slacker of the highest order. He's a good waiter, but he doesn't pitch in on jobs like cleaning up because he knows his tips don't depend on it. How do we make sure he does his share?

Key Words / Concepts: group incentives, withholding effort, free riding, self-managed teams, empowerment, norms

Discussion Points: Should the wait staff be given more responsibility considering the fact that Bill won't do his share? Why or why not? Whose responsibility is it to ensure that all members of a team are performing at acceptable levels? The management? The team members?

Related Reference: Anonymous (1995). How to prevent social loafing on teams. *Supervisory Management*, September, Vol.40, No.9, p.1.

Smokers

? Now that the Food and Drug Administration has classified nicotine as an addictive drug and is attempting to regulate it, can smoking and other uses of tobacco be classified as a disability under the ADA?

Key Words / Concepts: Americans with Disabilities Act (ADA), smoker's rights, second-hand smoke, drug and alcohol abuse, employee assistance program (EAP), off-the-job intrusion, health care costs

Discussion Points: What are the similarities and differences among cigarettes, marijuana, cocaine, and alcohol in relation to workplace policies and usage by employees? Should organizations refuse to hire smokers because they might increase health care costs and be absent because of illness more frequently? If members of some minority groups smoke more than other groups, would failure to hire smokers be considered disparate impact? Explain.

Related Reference: Woo, Jundo (1993). Employers fume over new legislation barring discrimination against smokers. *The Wall Street Journal*, June 4, p.B1-2.

Soliciting fellow employees for fund-raisers

? It seems like every time I turn around in our office, somebody is trying to sell me something to benefit their kid's fund-raiser. Girl Scout cookies, discount cards, Christmas paper, magazines, you name it and little Johnny's dad or mom wants my support. I suppose I could just say no. But I also don't think the office is the appropriate place to solicit . . . particularly because it has become a daily occurrence. Help! Poinsettia sales are approaching soon.

Key Words / Concepts: social responsibility, social obligation, community service, fund-raisers

Discussion Points: If a company's mission includes engaging in socially responsible behavior, shouldn't it allow employees to solicit for charitable causes? Should all soliciting be banned from work? Does soliciting for the United Way at work constitute unreasonable pressure on employees to make contributions?

Related Reference: Bedard, Paul, Makovsky, David, & Walsh, Kenneth T. (1999). Lighten up. *U.S. News & World Report*, April 12, Vol.126, p.5.

Strategy & HRM

I read all of these articles in the trade journals about fitting human resource management into the strategic planning of the organization. I was just hired as HR director of a company with 300 employees and an HR staff of four. There was a great deal of discussion in my job interviews about this linkage between HR and top management. They seemed raring to go with these ideas. When I talked informally with my predecessor, who is moving to another company, she wished me luck in getting involved in strategic planning. She had been unable to do so in her six years as HR director; HR was seen as a tool of the planners to make their plans happen. I took the job anyway. Do you have any suggestions for establishing and improving the linkage between the top managers and the HR department?

Key Words / Concepts: strategic planning, corporate strategy, business strategy, functional strategy, strategic human resource management, staff function, line function

Discussion Points: What does competitive advantage mean? How can effective human resource management be a source of sustained competitive advantage? What are some of the difficulties in being involved in an organization's strategic planning when one holds a staff position?

Related Reference: Barney, Jay B. & Wright, Patrick M. (1998). On becoming a strategic partner: The role of human resources in gaining competitive advantage. *Human Resource Management*, Vol.37, p.31-46.

Succession planning

A recent plane crash in which a group of top executives were killed made me a bit concerned about succession planning and what would happen to my company if I died or one of my key employees died. My company has fewer than 100 employees. Do you think a company of this size needs such a plan?

Key Words / Concepts: management development, succession planning, human resource information system, management replacement chart, coaching, business strategy

Discussion Points: Is succession planning only cost effective in large organizations? How should succession planning occur in a small family business?

Related Reference: Borwick, C. (1993). Eight ways to assess succession plans. *HRMagazine*, May, p.109-114.

T

Team building

My company was experiencing a great deal of turmoil so I brought a consultant in to provide exercises in building effective teams. Now I have two teams in my company: the employees are on one team and I'm on the other. Productivity is worse than ever; we're fighting all of the time. What did I do wrong?

Key Words / Concepts: team building, group cohesion, self-directed teams, empowerment, training, communication

Discussion Points: Should every organization move toward the use of teams? What are the pros and cons of using team building in the organization? How involved should management be in the process of building teams within the organization?

Related Reference: Fischetti, Mark (1998). Team doctors, report to ER!, *Fast Company*, February-March, Vol.13, p.170-177.

Theft & forgiveness

I recently caught one of my very valuable, highly skilled workers stealing from me. He was caught "red handed." He admitted what he had done, and I immediately fired him. The problem is that I can't find a similarly qualified replacement. His skills were top notch and very specialized. He came to me two months later, begging for forgiveness and his old job back. Given that I'm having such a difficult time filling this very critical position, I'm tempted to hire him back. But I'm afraid of the message I may be sending. Any advice?

Key Words / Concepts: job rotation, talent inventories, cross-training, recruiting, disciplinary process

Discussion Points: How could the current situation have been avoided long before the employee was caught stealing? How would other employees react if the thief was rehired?

Related Reference: O'Reilly, C. A.,III, & Weitz, B. A. (1980). Managing marginal employees: The use of warnings and dismissals. *Administrative Science Quarterly*, Vol.25, p. 467-484.

Theft prevention

I own a small business with seven employees. One of the seven has worked for me less than three months and replaced a woman I was forced to let go. I have found that one of my employees has been stealing between $100 and $200 a month from me over the course of a year. I can't prove anything, but because the thefts seemed to stop when my one ex-employee was fired, I suspect it was her. Is there anything I can do?

Key Words / Concepts: auditing, internal controls, checks and balances, perceived fairness, paper trail

Discussion Points: Now that the thefts have stopped, should the owner do anything? Should the owner pursue the ex-employee to seek restitution for the money that was taken? What might the owner do to protect against future theft?

Related Reference: Taylor, Robert R., & Prien, Kristen O. (1998). Preventing employee theft: A behavioral approach. *Business Perspectives*, Vol.10, No.4, p.9-13.

Tokenism

I recently received an invitation from corporate headquarters asking me to take part in a management task force on training needs for employees at our various company divisions. My excellent work record was cited as the main reason for inviting me to be on the task force. I met with a staff person from the headquarters last week and during the course of the conversation, she told me she was so happy I would be part of the group because the company really wanted some better information on how to train its "multicultural" workforce.

I happen to be an African-American woman, and I was extremely hurt and insulted at what she said. I thought they were including me because I was an excellent employee. Now I don't know what to believe. Should I take part in the task force? Should I complain to someone?

Key Words / Concepts: workplace diversity, discrimination, Title VII, training needs assessment, management development, group decision making

Discussion Points: Evaluate the facts presented in this question and determine whether this is a potential case of discrimination. How should a human resource manager attempt to ensure that all of its organizational task forces and other groups have a membership that will provide information about all aspects of the problem at hand?

Related Reference: Strach, Lauren and Wicander, Linda (1993). Fitting in: Issues of tokenism and conformity for minority women. *SAM Advanced Management Journal*, Summer, Vol.58, No.3, p.22-25.

Tongue rings & tattoos

? I've got an employee who is a hard worker, with a good attitude, but he's always been a bit on the bizarre side. Today, he came into work with a pierced ring in his tongue. What can I do about this? Are there any legal ramifications if I choose to terminate him?

Key Words / Concepts: body jewelry, dress codes, BFOQ, Title VII, diversity

Discussion Point: Is an organization that claims to encourage diversity, yet has a strict dress code, being hypocritical?

Related Reference: Lynn, Jacqueline (1998). War and pierce: Setting policies on facial jewelry and body art, *Entrepreneur*, June, Vol.26 No.6 p.104.

Tuition reimbursement

? We have had a program at our company where we pay tuition for employees who want to take courses that will help them in their jobs.

I may be old and cynical, but I can't see that the program benefits the company in any way. Half of those taking course work rush out of the office to get to night classes, when they need to be focusing 150 percent on the work of the company. The other half we've paid to put through school have quit and taken better-paying jobs.

Isn't it the responsibility of the employee to get the education required for the job he wants? When kids are graduating from high school, are we going to have to hire them immediately and pay their way through $100,000 worth of school just so we can increase their salaries in time for them to leave for another employer?

Key Words / Concepts: education, tuition reimbursement programs, employee development, management development, cost–benefit analysis, lifelong learning

Discussion Points: Which types of employees would be best suited to participate in tuition assistance programs? What could line managers do to benefit from their employees' participation in such programs? Do you think turnover at this company would decrease if these programs were eliminated? Why or why not?

Related Reference: Dupont, Dale K. (1999). Tuition aid that can make the grade. *HRMagazine*, April, Vol.44, No.4, p.74-80.

Turnover

Over the past year, our company has had what I feel is a very high turnover rate. I hired seven people last year and only two are left. Although it's been a particular problem in our entry-level positions, I recently lost four senior people as well. I'm spending an inordinate amount of time rehiring and retraining, when I really need to be focusing on other areas of the company. I can't attribute the problem to bad hiring decisions on my part, because these were all employees I valued. Some had been loyal employees for years. Do you have any suggestions for reducing the turnover?

Key Words / Concepts: exit interviews, realistic job previews, compensation policies, internal labor markets, organizational culture

Discussion Points: Is turnover necessarily a bad thing? Why or why not? How can an organization determine its turnover costs? What is an "acceptable" turnover rate? How can compensation strategies, culture, and career paths be used to limit turnover?

Related Reference: Middlebrook, John, F. (1999). Avoiding Brain Drain: How to lock in talent. *HR Focus*, March, Vol.41, No.5 p.511-525.

U

Unemployment compensation

One of my best employees just walked in and told me she was giving her two weeks' notice. I was further shocked to learn she would be opening a business that would directly compete with me. I was angry, as well as concerned, that if she stayed on during the remaining two weeks she would

steal my customers. So I told her two weeks' notice was not necessary and that she should clear out her desk on the spot. She became furious and said that she was counting on the two weeks' pay for her business start-up. She argued that if I was forcing her to leave now, she was not quitting; she was being fired. Can she collect unemployment or sue me for improper termination? This is not fair.

Key Words / Concepts: termination, wrongful discharge, public policy exceptions, dismissal procedures, termination interview, noncompete clause, unemployment insurance

Discussion Points: Evaluate the appropriateness of requiring employees at the time of hiring to sign an agreement not to quit and go to work for a competitor for a period of one year after termination. For which level of employee, if any, would such an agreement seem appropriate?

Related Reference: Falcone, Paul (1999). Resignations. *HRMagazine*, April, Vol.44, No.4, p.124-126.

Union comfort level

I'm the human resource manager in a union company, and our management is committed to maintaining good union–management relations. My job requires me to interview applicants for positions that are represented by the union. I want to make sure that anyone we hire will fit in to our strong union environment. Would it be legal and proper for me to ask applicants about whether they have previously worked in union shops to help us gauge whether the applicant will be suited to work here?

Key Words / Concepts: person–organization fit, collective bargaining, labor–management relations, employee commitment

Discussion Points: Are there any legal areas of inquiry that a nonunion employer could pursue to determine if an applicant is pro-union? If so, what are they, and how would you recommend that an employer broach them in the selection interview?

Related Reference: Segal, Jonathan A. (1992). The "u" word. *HRMagazine*, August, Vol. 37, No.8, p.89-90

V

Violence at work

 Recent television news programs have indicated that it is no longer safe to be at work. By all accounts, it seems that disgruntled postal workers aren't the only ones who have resorted to resolving their differences by shooting co-workers and supervisors. How can I protect my employees and myself from being attacked on the job?

Key Words / Concepts: workplace violence, security, employee screening, discipline, violence training, job stress, burnout

Discussion Points: How does the organization balance security precautions with the ability of employees to have the freedom to do their jobs effectively? At what point should a line manager involve human resources and others if an employee discusses possible violent behavior or if the manager hears of a threat made by an employee?

Related Reference: Neuman, Joel H. & Baron, Robert A. (1998). Workplace violence and workplace aggression: Evidence concerning specific forms, potential causes and preferred targets. *Journal of Management*, Vol.24, p.391-419.

W

Weather, storms, & natural disasters

We are having difficulty deciding how to handle compensating our employees for work during a recent ice storm. Because of our location in a southern state, the storm's severity was unprecedented. Some employees came to work and stayed the entire day; other employees had to leave early to pick up their children from school; and other employees did not make it to work at all because of icy conditions. Our company could not close its operations during the bad weather. Should we penalize the employees who did not work during the ice storm?

Key Words / Concepts: absenteeism, compensation, procedural fairness, equity theory

Discussion Points: What will be the reaction of the employees to this decision? What should you do if you hear that one of the employees who couldn't come to work believed he might have been injured if he had tried to do so?

Related Reference: Zachary, Mary-Kathryn (1997). Weather-related discipline. *SuperVision*, August, Vol.58, No.8, p. 9-20.

Work relationships & "getting along"

I have recently terminated an employee because I felt that her working and professional relationships with her superiors and a few of her peers were going quickly in the wrong direction. Her job performance was outstanding, as far as her technical work was concerned. However, she had bad working relationships with both her team and other managers with whom she came in contact at our company. In my opinion, she was not fitting into the new, dynamic organization we are attempting to build. She would not handle multiple tasks. She was inflexible and definitely opposed teamwork. My problem is that I'm having some angst over what I feel was a subjective and vague reason on my part for termination . . . particularly given her technical job performance. She immediately received an offer for employment from one of our competitors, which makes me feel even worse about my decision. Was I out of line to focus on her inability to "get along"?

Thanks God, for providing me with such charming co-workers

Key Words / Concepts: organizational culture, realistic job previews, person–organization fit, technical skills, social skills, soft skills

Discussion Points: What is the relative importance of technical skills versus social skills in the workplace? Which types of jobs might put greater stress on social skills? Would workplaces that practice quality management be more likely to place greater emphasis on technical skills or social skills, or an equal emphasis on each? Explain.

Related Reference: Montgomery, Clifford E. (1996). Organizational fit is key to job success. *HRMagazine*, January, Vol.41, No.1, p.94-96.

X

"X" generation

 We frequently pass articles from business magazines that might be of interest around the office. Two articles that circulated in the office last week focused on how to manage "generation X" employees and posed the pros and cons of hiring "Xers" as managers.

As a 31-year-old who meets the age requirements to be classified as part of "generation X," I am offended by the sweeping generalizations as to how I will manage my employees and what I'm looking for in an organization. I am particularly offended because one of the articles was from *HRMagazine*, a journal for the so-called enlightened human resource professional.

What these articles are doing doesn't seem too different to me than someone stereotyping the work habits and attitudes of blacks, older workers, women, or gays. I'm sure if I remotely suggested ways in which members of these groups behaved or should be managed, my HR professional would help me clean out my desk. What is going on?

Key Words / Concepts: stereotypes, trend analysis, diversity, demographics, workforce composition

Discussion Points: Why should managers be concerned with trends in workforce diversity? How can we use demographic data and workforce trends without inappropriately stereotyping individuals?

Related Reference: Adams III, John T. (1999). But what about gen xers who manage boomers? *HRMagazine*, December., Vol.44, No.13, p.8.

X & Y management

About six months ago, our organization aligned territories, necessitating some shuffling of our office management. One of the office managers, who was extremely beloved by his employees and who thought the best of his team, was transferred out and replaced by an individual with several years of supervisory experience and a strong background in our industry. Since the day this new manager joined us, he's done nothing but complain about how lazy and untrustworthy the employees are under his direction. He claims that none of them know what they're doing and that if he didn't constantly stay on top of them nothing would ever get done. I had basically ignored his complaints given that the previous manager had awarded these same employees outstanding performance reviews and given that the department's performance measures are slightly above where they were this time last year.

Today my new manager presented me with several documented cases of insubordination among his employees. To make matters worse, one of these "insubordinate" individuals had been nominated as our organization's outstanding employee of the year in 1995. He stated that none of his employees are willing to work overtime; and he brought to my attention two individuals who have been abusing both their break time and sick leave. He wants to fire the whole bunch and with the evidence, I'm not sure I blame him. It just seems odd that two managers could have such contrasting views of the same employees or that these employees would change so quickly. Could it be that the previous manager was just doing that lousy of a job of performance evaluation or for some reason covering for his staff?

Key Words / Concepts: Theory X and Theory Y, self-fulfilling prophecy, Pygmalion effect, halo effect, leniency, strictness, alternation ranking method, critical incident method

Discussion Points: List and evaluate the factors that may have led to the very different performance appraisals delivered by the two managers.

Related Reference: Livingston, Sterling J. (1988). Pygmalion in management. *Harvard Business Review,* Sept.-Oct., Vol.66, No.5, p.121-129.

Xenophobia

My company is starting an international operation and we need to send a manager/salesperson into Mexico to make contacts and get the operation going. Our top performer, Patrick, is a great salesman who is also a very good manager. We think he could do a great job because of these skills and also because he actually had three years of Spanish in college and can speak the language fluently. Our problem is that Patrick is very anti-immigration and constantly makes disparaging comments about Latin America, specifically Mexico and illegal immigrants. We believe he does not like foreigners because of these comments, but we think he's best for the job. What should we do?

Key Words / Concepts: expatriate manager, ethnocentrism, parochialism, national culture, diversity, cultural toughness, others orientation

Discussion Points: What factors should be considered in appointing a person to an expatriate position in a foreign country whose culture is quite different from the United States'? What kinds of traits should be sought in such a manager during the selection process? How could a person be trained to be successful in an expatriate position?

Related Reference: Solomon, C.M. (1994). Success abroad depends on more than job skills. *Personnel Journal*, April, Vol.73, No.4, p.51-60.

─────────────── **Y** ───────────────

"Yellow dog" contracts

When I reported for work at my new summer job for a small family restaurant, the owner asked me to sign a paper that said I was not a union member and

that I had no plans to join a union while I worked at the company. She said she had trouble with union people last summer and didn't want to hire anyone who might try to start a union at the restaurant. Is this sort of document legally binding? Why would the company do this?

Key Words / Concepts: Norris-LaGuardia Act, Wagner Act, National Labor Relations Board, unfair labor practices, authorization cards, preventive employee relations

Discussion Points: As a human resource manager, how would you advise your company to stay union free and do so legally and ethically? Evaluate strategies an employer can use to defeat a union election.

Related Reference: Segal, Jonathan. (1998). Unshackle your supervisors to stay union-free. *HRMagazine*, June, Vol.43, No.7, p.177-185.

Z

Zero defects

Our president recently gave a speech to the troops and stressed the importance of the company instituting a zero-defects culture as its major strategic goal for the year. His "vision" was for our company to be viewed as having the highest quality in our industry. We were not to produce or ship any product with a defect that could even possibly cause its return by the customer.

I certainly had no problem with his "vision." However, about a week later, we received a memo, also from the top dog, asking us to submit suggested budget cuts in our departments of 10 percent over the next year.

The other managers and I talked to each other, and we agreed privately that we need those resources in order to realize the strategic vision of a zero-defects culture. How can we get to zero defects if we cut our budgets?

Key Words / Concepts: total quality management, strategic planning, zero-defects culture, empowerment, vision, organizational change, organizational culture, leadership

Discussion Points: Can a program to attain the goal of zero defects in manufacturing exist at the same time as a cost-reduction program? If so, under what circumstances? Identify ways that a human resource manager can help the chief executive officer realize an organization's vision.

Related Reference: Ngin, P. M. & Chong, Chee Leong (1997). Achieving zero defects. *Employee Relations*, Vol.19, p.374-387.

A

Absenteeism

 The supervisor is making a medical judgment when he suggests that if the employee is too sick to do her job, then she is also too sick to do anything else. If questioned, the employee and the physician might very well argue that attending the workshop was nonstressful . . . even therapeutic, while performing her job duties that day may have been viewed as stressful. Hence, unless you have some policy that excludes staff on sick leave from attending such events, you have little basis for action.

Is the employee a poor performer? Has there been a pattern of excessive absenteeism? Does this person have a history of trying to get away with things? You may attack her absences, coupled with her overall work performance record. However, abuse, which implies dishonesty, does not seem to be established in this case.

The sick leave incident seems to point to a deeper problem between the supervisor and the employee in question and an overall problem with the employee's level of job satisfaction. First, you have a supervisor "staking out" a company event so as to catch the culprit in the act of attending. Second, you have an employee with a stress-related diagnosis, which you think is related to her work environment. Finally, you have an unnamed company-sponsored workshop that the employee was told she could not attend. We suspect that the topic of the workshop might prove to be your most important clue as to what is going on here. Whatever it was, it was important to her.

Employee withdrawal actions such as chronic or unauthorized absenteeism and stress- related absenteeism are closely linked to employee job dissatisfaction. Job satisfaction tends to be highest among those employees who believe their supervisors are competent, treat them with respect, and have their best interests in mind. Job satisfaction is enhanced when there are open lines of communication between the supervisor and the employee. We suggest that you look closely at the employee's perceptions of the quality of supervision. Keep in mind that paying people fairly, decentralizing decision making, and matching people to jobs that are in line with their interests also enhance job satisfaction and serve to reduce stress-related absences or nonlegitimate absences. However, given the information at hand, the working relationship between the supervisor and the employee should be closely examined.

It also may be useful to determine whether there is a problem with unauthorized absenteeism in this manager's area as a whole. That is, what is the rate of absenteeism in his department compared to other departments? Some managers are tougher to work for than others, and companies often track absenteeism rates by individual manager. This helps to identify isolated trouble spots that might be related to poor or ineffective management style.

This isn't to say that the employee in question has done nothing wrong or that the supervisor's management style is off base. The situation, as you have described it, does suggest that there is tension between the two and, if left alone, the two will have a difficult time constructively solving any related performance problem or expectation. The likely outcome will be that the employee will become so dissatisfied she'll quit. It may be that this is exactly what the supervisor wants. You need to know this. If, on the other hand, his goal is to retain a valuable employee, we suggest you or the department head become involved as a third-party mediator. Your role would then be primarily that of a facilitator, helping the two toward an acceptable solution.

Additional References:

Gellatly, Ian R. and Luchak, Andrew A. (1998). Personal and organizational determinants of perceived absence norms. *Human Relations*, August, Vol.51, No.8, p.1085-1103.

Kweller, Deborah S. (1998). The emerging model of absence management. *HR Focus*, August, Vol.75, No.8, p.9-10.

Accidents

 One way to reduce accidents is to screen out accident-prone people before they are hired. However, remember that the Americans with Disabilities Act (applicable to employers with 15 or more employees) has particular relevance for safety-related screening decisions. For example, in the past, many employers routinely asked about their job applicants' workers' compensation history. Under the ADA, this is an unlawful practice.

You can ask applicants whether they have the ability to perform a job or even ask, "Do you know of any reason why you would not be able to perform the various functions of the job you are seeking?" This is an important question because accident-proneness seems to be a function of the situation in which the individual is placed. Sure, we've all run across individuals we would consider accident-prone: always dropping things, bumping into doors, or falling. However, the constant accidents often are due to a mismatch between the individual and the job's functions. For certain functions, a high level of coordination may be important.

Similarly, a high level of emotional stability, the ability to work in distracting conditions, or a certain level of vision may be required. In a study conducted at a paper mill, 52 accident-free employees were compared with 52 accident-prone employees. It was found that 63 percent of the no-accident group passed a vision test, while only 33 percent of the accident-prone group passed. The bottom line is that, through better selection, managers can reduce accidents and improve the caliber of their employees at the same time.

Additional References:

Goldberg, Allan T. (1996). Finding the root causes of accidents. *Occupational Hazards*, November, Vol.58, No.11, p.33-39.

Neville, Haig (1998). Workplace accidents: They cost more than you think. *Industrial Management*, Jan./Feb., Vol.40, No.1, p.7-9.

Adult learners

We think your problem stems not so much from the short attention span of your trainees as it does from the conflict between your training methods and their learning styles. You have discovered the hard way that adults learn quite differently than your children do in school. Several researchers in learning theory call the different approach to adult learning "andragogy" in contrast with the more familiar term "pedagogy," which literally means the art and science of teaching children.

Andragogy has four basic assumptions that differ quite significantly from those of the pedagogical model of education. First, the andragogy model assumes that adults are self-directed. Second, adults have knowledge and experience that can be used as a learning resource. Third, adults have a greater readiness to learn things that relate to their jobs or other aspects of their lives. Finally, adults are motivated to learn so they can solve problems, and they expect to immediately apply what they have learned.

The safety material you wish to get across to these employees appears to address points three and four pretty well. Your employees want to learn material that helps them do their jobs, and they will apply that material to solve problems such as unsafe working conditions. However, you may need to adjust your teaching techniques and classroom atmosphere to make your learners feel more self-directed and involved in the learning process. One important strategy is changing the class format. Try paring down your detailed presentation, only transmitting essential information and then encouraging the employees to become involved in application discussions in small groups of three or four. They can discuss among themselves how the safety information might best be applied to their jobs. Such discussions might allow the learners to feel more self-directed and encourage them to bring their own knowledge and experience to the learning process.

After the small groups of employees discuss the material, you can reconvene the groups and have each group report on the major elements of their discussions. You might then fill in some points that you wish to make, ask for their reactions, and see where the discussion goes.

The key to teaching adult learners is to maintain flexibility and be responsive. This approach is enhanced by keeping a relaxed, informal, and supportive atmosphere rather than the formal, authority-oriented atmosphere you might recall from your school days. The employees will learn because they want to, not because you make them. Involving them in the process and tapping their knowledge will aid your efforts and make the employees feel more like partners in the learning experience. A two-way approach that encourages the learners to express their opinions and make suggestions on how to apply the material also provides you with feedback to adjust the sessions as necessary. A straight lecture or a mind-numbing barrage of PowerPoint slides will not lend itself to feedback to the instructor, other than glassy-eyed stares.

Additional References:

Hill, Janette R. & Hannafin, Michael J., (1997). Cognitive strategies and learning from the World Wide Web. *Educational Technology Research & Development*, Vol.45, No.4, p.37-66.

Zemke, Ron (1998). In search of self-directed learners. *Training*, May, Vol.35, No.5, p.60-68.

Alcohol abuse

 The Americans with Disabilities Act considers alcoholism to be a medical condition and, as such, a disability. Employers are prohibited from discriminating against employees solely because of diagnosed alcoholism.

Further, discipline or termination of the employee should be based on objective work-related issues, not on suspected or diagnosed alcoholism. So, if you suspect an alcohol abuse problem, you would want to document deteriorating conditions, such as absences from work and lowered quantity or quality of work and base the confrontation *only* on job performance. If the employee self-identifies alcoholism or drug addiction as the cause of the problem, you would seek a commitment from the employee to obtain professional help and to improve performance. All the while you would continue to monitor and document performance.

Keep in mind that what we've just described refers to confirmed or suspected off-duty abuse of alcohol that results in performance problems. What you've described is drinking and being under the influence of alcoholic beverages while on duty. In most organizations, this is cause for termination. At the very least, his intoxication prevented him from performing his job, in your eyes, and he should have been sent home.

Now that time has passed, you could still confront the employee with your observations of that day, including the slurred speech and alcohol on the breath, and then follow your organization's standard disciplinary procedures. Of course, as in other disciplinary actions, everything should be documented.

However, don't stop at this point. You noted in your question that because of the small size of your company, you don't have a specific written policy covering alcohol. Your firm may be small, but it clearly experiences the same problems of large firms, including drug and alcohol abuse. We encourage you to immediately address this issue with the company's owners and strengthen your policy manual. Let employees know that drug and alcohol use that affects job performance, workplace safety, or public liability is not permitted and explain what will happen if they violate the policy. Be sure to outline the use of alcohol at company-sponsored events and being under the influence while on the job. You'll also want to identify company resources where employees with alcohol problems can get help and to describe the responsibility of the employee to seek and complete treatment.

Sample policies and procedures may be obtained from the Department of Labor, through the National Clearinghouse for Alcohol and Drug Information at 1-800-729-6686 or online at http://www.health.org/workpl.htm.

You may think it ridiculous that employees don't understand the necessity of staying sober and the consequences of showing up to work drunk. Yet, recall that only a few years ago, the three-martini lunch was standard business fare.

Additional references:

King, Phyllis A. & Blalock, Mary B. (1998). Alcohol in the workplace: last call. *Supervision*, March, Vol.59, No.3, p.16-17.

Schweitzer, M. E.,& Kerr, J. (2000). Bargaining under the influence: The role of alcohol in negotiations. *The Academy of Management Executive*, May, Vol.14, No.2, p.47-57.

U.S. Department of Labor (1990). *An Employer's Guide to Dealing With Substance Abuse*. October.

Alcohol & the office party

Company parties can be a good way to show appreciation, bolster morale, and increase work team cohesiveness. However, as your colleague points out, they also can result in undesirable outcomes . . . legal and otherwise. Many organizations have eliminated alcohol from their parties or have stopped sponsoring parties entirely. Some are concerned about the possibility alcohol consumption may lead to increased incidents of sexual harassment when employees "let their hair down" at such functions. Others fear the possibility of increased on-site injury (e.g., falling down drunk) or fear the employee may be involved in an accident on the way home.

If alcohol is served, you should not fail to take care of an employee who becomes intoxicated. It may not be the employer's responsibility to ensure that the staff does not get drunk, but when the partygoers are unable to look after themselves, the employer must take over. Be sure to provide the individual who's had a bit too much Christmas cheer with transportation home. If an employee must return to work after the party, make certain it is understood that the consumption of any alcoholic beverage at the party is strictly forbidden.

While you are still in the planning stages, check your company's liability insurance. Chances are good that any on-premises events are covered, but it may be advisable to purchase additional event-specific insurance. Avoid kegs and punch that may invite unlimited drinking and mask the amount of alcohol being consumed. Never have a low-level employee or nonmanagement person serve liquor. Such employees may not be able to effectively refuse to serve a high-level manager who is drinking too much. Hiring a professional catering company to tend bar may serve to eliminate this delicate situation.

While mixing alcohol and mistletoe at a company function can create serious problems, these suggestions may lessen your worries and prevent the Grinch from stealing the holiday "spirits" from your party. Cheers!

Additional references:

Atkinson, Lynn (1996). Don't let legal problems spoil holiday parties *HR Focus*, December, Vol.73, No.12, P.14.

Caggiano, Christopher (1997). Cancel the Christmas party. *Inc.*, December, Vol.19,No.18, p160-161.

B

Battered & abused coworker

Many larger organizations have formal programs that provide employees with referral and counseling in such cases where personal problems spill into the workplace. It is estimated that 50 percent of employers with 500 or more employees have access to an employee assistance program (EAP) for problems such as abuse, alcoholism, gambling addiction, or stress. However, as a small organization without an EAP, there are still several alternatives depending upon how comfortable you are with becoming involved in an employee's personal life. Although it is tempting to stand up for an employee who is possibly being abused and urge her to go to the authorities, it is important for you to approach this situation— initially at least—as a performance problem. You should focus on the employee's late arrival to work and the effect this has on the efficiency of the office. On the one hand, you want the abuse of tardiness and absences to stop. On the other hand, you do not want to invade the employee's privacy by prying too deeply into the reasons for her coming to work late.

First, let her know that the lateness and frequent absences cannot be tolerated and leave the door open for her to bring up the out-of-office abuse as an excuse for her shortcomings at work. If she does not bring it up, focus exclusively on the performance problem and the consequences, if no satisfactory improvement is forthcoming.

If she does bring abuse up, you can urge her to seek counseling or assistance from a local agency such as the YWCA Family Violence & Sexual Assault Center. An alternative would be to actively help the woman by contacting the authorities and arranging some other form of support or shelter from the abusive situation. However, such activities could put you at personal risk from the boyfriend and certainly could be interpreted as excessive prying. Yet, you may find it to be an appropriate approach from an ethical standpoint. In addition, we view physical abuse as a crime that should be reported.

Ultimately, what you do as a manager depends a great deal upon your sense of values and how much you care about an employee who may be suffering from an intolerable situation. These concerns must be balanced with the employee's rights of privacy, the needs of your business, and your own well-being.

Additional References:

Cohen, Gary S. & Gard, Lawrence H. (1998). Employee assistance programs: A preventive, cost-effective benefit. *Journal of Health Care Finance*, Spring, Vol.24, No.3, p45-53.

Meier, Barry (1996). When abuse follows women to work. *New York Times*, March 10, p.11.

Pereira, Joseph (1995). Employers confront domestic abuse. *Wall Street Journal -- Eastern Edition*, March 2, 1995, p.B1.

Beepers, pagers, & cell phones

 To stop this harassment, your company should institute "on-call" periods for evenings and weekends for those who are provided with pagers by the company. If your organization does not have a pager policy, you should discuss establishing one immediately with your boss and the human resources director. The policy should set forth the purposes of the paging system, proper uses of the pager, who may use the pager, and designated "on-call" periods. If on-call periods are established, you should not be paged when you are not on-call.

Other policy considerations include employee expectations of privacy when they are using the pager. Federal and state laws concerning restrictions and requirements of the paging system should be reviewed. If the company plans to monitor the use of the pager, it is wise for the company to disclose this fact. Employees also should be told that, as a matter of policy, inappropriate, personal, or discriminatory messages are prohibited.

Explain to your boss that you are finding the beeper abuse very stressful and that several employees are contacting you regarding trivial and nonwork-related matters. You might mention Aesop's fable about the boy who cried wolf and add that you are afraid you will discount a real emergency call due to all of these unimportant calls.

Ask the boss to immediately establish on-call periods for managers and publicize those on-call periods to employees. For your part, you should report the abuse of these periods and of other elements of the policy. If the harassment continues, you may have to turn in the beeper and tell your boss that it is adversely affecting your job performance.

Additional References:

Bennett, Steven C. & Locke, Stuart D. (1998). Privacy in the workplace: A practical primer. *Labor Law Journal*, Vol.49, p.781-787.

Donlan, Thomas G. (1996). Who's calling? *Barron's*, April, Vol.76, No.14, p.54.

Hubbartt, William S. (1998). *The new battle over workplace privacy*, New York: American Management Association, p.148-151, 159.

Belligerence

 It's certainly true that Joe was rude to you at this meeting, but your situation reminds us of the old saying, "You've made your bed, now lie in it." You and the president set up ground rules for this meeting: anything goes. One of the employees took you at your word; now you want to fire him for telling you what you did not want to hear!

Next time think about establishing effective ground rules first, and do so in cooperation with the employees. At the start of the meeting, you should ask the employees for their thoughts on establishing appropriate conduct for the meeting. Some suggested ground rules might be (1) no speeches (2) no attacks on individuals, (3) no discussions of personal matters, and (4) time limit on discussing any one issue. These rules may not have stopped Joe's attacks, but at least they would have given you a way to get the meeting back on track.

The president is right. If you fire Joe because he attacked you, you will create more difficulties for the company. Even though his conduct probably rises to the level of insubordination, he was set up by the lack of rules at the meeting. The other employees will notice he was fired for speaking his mind at your invitation. Firing him will escalate ill will in the organization and negatively affect the morale and productivity of the other workers.

Joe's diatribe indicates some serious communication problems at your organization, particularly in the flow of unsubstantiated rumors throughout the plant. What you can do about the larger issue seems an appropriate question. One solution that might help would be to more actively monitor and influence the company grapevine, or informal communication channels. You and other managers need to communicate more with employees on a personal basis to find out the kind of information that is being passed around the organization outside formal communication channels. Research indicates that the grapevine generally spreads information accurately as long as the information is easy to understand and relevant to those involved. Sometimes the information is incorrect, as in the example Joe cited.

As a manager, you can monitor inaccurate information being spread through the grapevine and use either the informal channel or a formal announcement to put out the correct story. In doing so, you must not violate the privacy of any employee or otherwise behave unethically. But if you heard that employees believe the company provided a raise to an employee who was threatening to quit, you could informally, through your supervisors, put out the fact—if true—that the company does not raise pay when employees threaten to leave. The first step in monitoring and influencing the grapevine is to meet with supervisors and discuss how important it is for them to pass along to you what they hear on the shop floor. You and the senior managers can then respond to these rumors, if necessary.

Additional references:

Driscoll, Dawn Marie & Hoffman, Michael W. (1997). Allow employees to speak out on company practices. Workforce, November, p.73-76.

Hickey, John V. & Casner-Lotto, Jill (1998). How to get true employee participation. *Training & Development,* Vol.52, No.2, p.58-61.

Kennedy, Marilyn Moats (1998). The new rules of leadership and organizational politics. *Manager's Intelligence Report,* January, p.8.

C

Casual clothing

 Casual dress in the workplace is gaining widespread popularity in organizations throughout the country. In a recent survey of organizations where casual dress is allowed, the vast majority of employees with these organizations felt that dressing casually had a variety of benefits beyond comfort. Many of the respondents said when dressed casually they felt more camaraderie with managers and co-workers and that supervisors appeared more approachable. Forty-one percent felt casual dress improved worker productivity, while only 4 percent perceived a negative impact. However, it is important to note that this survey, along with many with similar findings, is paid for by the casual apparel industry.

In addition, casual dress at some buttoned-down companies can be somewhat of a shock to corporate culture. Implementing a casual dress policy slowly, temporarily (such as in the heat of summer), or occasionally provides employees, management, and customers time to become accustomed to the idea of casual business-wear. It also gives each group a chance to find the parameters of what is acceptable and what isn't. As far as the importance of dressing for success—casual days don't mean slob days. If you want to prevent casual-wear better suited to the beach than the office from entering the workplace, decide ahead on guidelines for what is and is not appropriate casual-wear, periodically remind employees about appropriate standards, and, when dealing with a "problem" employee, be gentle. Clothes can be a touchy issue.

Additional reference:

Biecher, Elisa, Keaton, Paul N. & Pollman, William A. (1999). Casual dress at work. *SAM Advanced Management Journal*, Winter, Vol.64, p.17-20.

Change

 Like Roy, we are all creatures of habit. We often have a tendency to resist such major changes as you describe because these transformations represent a real or imagined threat to an established work routine. Many employees resist change because of a fear of the unknown, a fear of failure, a loss of status or job security, peer pressure, or the existence of mistrust between management and employees. To many people, modernization means replacement of person with machine, and this is not always true.

Possible strategies to cope with employee resistance to change include

- Providing as much information as possible to employees about the change.
- Informing employees about the reason for the change.
- Helping them see the logic of making the change.
- Conducting meetings to clarify employee questions regarding the change.

- Providing employees with an opportunity to discuss how the proposed change might affect them.
- Giving them input into the change process and compromise, if possible.

These suggestions are effective, but because they are costly and time-consuming, some businesses tend not to use them. Instead, some companies might manipulate employees into accepting the changes or co-opt the major resistors by appointing them to committees involved with implementing the change. As a last resort, companies use coercion, direct threats of dismissal that could ultimately undermine the credibility of the proposed change. We suggest that you ask Roy's co-workers to help you educate Roy about the need for the change and communicate to him that these changes are designed to enhance his work life, not cost him his job.

Offering support in getting him up to speed on the new equipment would be beneficial. When introducing a new technology or equipment modernization to employees who have had a set routine for many years, it is valuable to provide hands-on experience with the new equipment and enlighten employees about the benefits of the new technology, how it will make their jobs much easier.

The surprisingly large number of individuals in the workplace who are functionally illiterate has created an even more complex barrier to change implementation. These employees have learned their jobs and can perform them blindfolded. However, when the job changes, they can't read the instruction manual that comes with that new piece of equipment. What appears to be an employee's resistance to adopt a new set of procedures may actually be an attempt to keep his/her inability to read a secret. Therefore, education may be needed in basic skills such as reading and math, as well as the more specific job skill training common in most companies.

If you feel that you have made a good faith effort to educate, communicate, and support Roy, and he still resists, you may have no alternative but to let him go. It is important, though, that you demonstrate to your workforce that you have gone the extra mile for Roy before taking such a drastic step.

Additional references:

Kotter, John (1995). Leading change: Why transformation efforts fail. Harvard Business Review, Vol.69, No.3, p.151-164.

Mariotti, John (1998). The challenge of change. *Industry Week*. April 6, Vol.247,No.7, p.140.

Commission sales

 Commission plans have several advantages over other plans. Sales costs are proportional to sales rather than being fixed, the company's selling investment is reduced, and it does motivate volume selling.

However, the commission plan also has drawbacks. Salespeople may focus only on high-volume items. On straight commission, salespeople also may neglect nonselling duties, or neglect cultivating new customers. In addition, pay is often excessive or very low, depending on the time of year or business cycle.

To determine whether commissions will serve as the best incentive for this new position, you also should consider the following: Will the compensation plan attract the right individual? How do your competitors pay their equivalent positions? Will there be a base salary? Will the price and/or volume change over the life of the product, and how will this affect sales compensation?

The most prevalent approach to sales compensation is to use a combination of salary and commissions to eliminate as many of the negatives of straight commission as possible. For any type of incentive plan to work, output must be measured easily and employees must be able to control their volume of output.

Additional references:

Anonymous (1993). Sales and service. *Small Business Reports*, July, Vol.18, No.7, p.43.

McCausland, Richard (1992). Marshall ends commissions; rivals wary. *Electronic News*, September 7, Vol.38, No.1928, p1.

Tallitsch, John & Moynahan, John (1994). Fine tuning sales compensation programs. *Compensation and Benefits Review*, March-April, Vol.29, No.2, p.34-37.

Complaints & excuses

 Individuals often attempt to present themselves in a positive way to influence and gain advantage with their bosses and coworkers. This is termed impression management. However, researchers Thomas Becker and Scott Martin suggest that impression management can go in the opposite direction: individuals might try to look bad at work on purpose, perhaps as a means to avoid additional tasks, responsibilities, or stress. Employees can do this by engaging in various behaviors such as absence, tardiness, faked illness, and long coffee breaks, or by telling others about their physical limitations, lack of skills or abilities, or other problems that constrain effective job performance.

Examples uncovered by the researchers include a computer operator who feigned incompetence to avoid being picked to work on a holiday, military personnel who did not display special abilities so they could elude enlistment for duties above and beyond their full-time jobs, and a sales clerk who skipped work to try and make her boss angry enough to cut her hours after he had earlier refused to do so. It is important to note in all of these examples that performance never falls below minimal acceptable standards that would lead to the individual's termination. They're just not giving the job all that they could.

As to Frank, you should observe his actions a little more closely to determine if he is actually slacking off on the job or if he is just *talking* about how poorly he is doing. Also, does he engage in this negative chatter around the boss or just to you and other co-workers? The person who tries to look bad at work has his reasons. These might include evading additional work, appearing overworked or stressed to merit a raise from a sensitive boss, and manipulating others in the organization by playing dumb.

After observing Frank, you may find that his performance is not really declining, but he is just putting on a show for the boss. If so, go about your job and attempt to ignore his braying. His negative impression management techniques are directed elsewhere. However, if his whining seems to be directed at you alone, he may be attempting to manipulate you into doing his work for him. You may benefit from either ignoring him or joining in the game and telling him how overworked you are and how much strain and stress you are suffering. Maybe he will stop playing and get back to work, but it may escalate to the point where you have to take up the problem with your supervisor because it is having a negative impact on your work.

Finally, attempt to do your own job without picking up slack for Frank. At times, when a co-worker is not working at full pace, we strive to compensate for his or her poor performance by increasing our own efforts. This is particularly true when the success of our own job depends on how well the co-worker is performing. If you must depend on Frank to do your job well, you should inform the supervisor if his constant complaining is adversely affecting your performance. You don't want your own performance appraisal to suffer due to Frank's antics.

Additional references:

Mulvey, Paul W., Bowes-Sperry, Lynn, & Klein, Howard J. (1998). The effects of perceived loafing and defensive impression management on group effectiveness. *Small Group Research*, Vol.29, p.394-415.

Rao, Asha & Schmidt, Stuart M. (1995). Upward impression management: Goals, influence strategies and consequences. *Human Relations*, Vol.48, p.147-166.

Corporate culture

 It is particularly important that your employees understand the need for changing the way they've been doing business. Why should they take risks? After all, your organization has been the market leader.

In addition, old habits are hard to break, and if your employees are accustomed to a paternalistic style of management that encouraged conservative decision making, you may need more than "talk" to get the participation, the risk taking, and the innovation that you desire. For example, in what way does your reward system encourage risk taking and participation? If one of your employees sticks his neck out, will it be chopped off when the outcome is less than desirable? Who gets rewarded or punished and why unequivocally states the organization's values and the expectations of its leadership.

Also, be aware that if you want individuals to take a riskier course of action, people tend to be risk seeking or risk averse based on how a problem is presented to them. Specifically, researchers have noted that problems presented in a manner that emphasizes the positive gains to be received from a course of action tend to encourage conservative decisions. Problems presented in a manner that emphasizes potential losses to be suffered lead to riskier decisions.

Finally, understand that some individuals possess a more risk-averse than risk-seeking personality. It may be that those with a more risk-seeking personality were made to feel uncomfortable under the old management and have long gone. If this is the case, you may need to inject a little new blood into the organization to model the behaviors you desire.

Additional references:

Kerr, Jeffrey & Slocum, John W., Jr. (1987). Managing corporate culture through reward systems. *The Academy of Management Executive*, May, Vol. 2, No. 2, p.99-107.

Shirley, Ian (1997). Playing it safe is a serious risk in sales promotion. *Marketing*, January 9, p.16.

D

Dating clients

First of all, you are assuming this accusation is true. It could be that the customer and the salesman are attempting to discredit Jennifer, who is apparently doing quite well at her job in a male-dominated field, by circulating unsubstantiated rumors. The customer might have asked her out, been rebuffed, and is now seeking revenge. The salesman may be grasping at the rumor to avoid targeting his own lackluster performance.

At any rate, it's time to use your network to determine if there is anything to the rumors involving Jennifer and to take corrective action if necessary. Discreetly contact other customers and salespeople to ask their opinions about the reasons for Jennifer's sales success. You might want to accompany Jennifer on a sales call to observe her techniques so you can make your own determination as to whether she knows the products and the pitch or whether some other factors might be involved in her accomplishments.

In sales, there is a thin line between socializing and dating. Perhaps your salesman is misinterpreting what Jennifer is doing. In this case, it is wise not to confront the employee until you have more information about what is actually going on. If your fact-finding leads you to believe the accusations are true, you then have to decide if you want your company's name besmirched by this sort of activity.

If Jennifer denies the accusations and is offended by your decision to confront her, she may quit. If Jennifer admits to sleeping with customers and sees nothing wrong with the practice, then what? Do you let Jennifer stay and continue to deal with ugly rumors and a blemished company reputation? Do you fire Jennifer and risk her being hired by a competitor who wants to take away your business? It's a classic ethical dilemma: Either choice has potentially negative consequences. We'll let you decide this individual case, but the eventual step may be to consider a policy that establishes proper conduct in these sorts of matters.

Additional references:

Anonymous (1996). Ticklish questions. *Across the Board*, April, Vol.33, No.4, p.46.

Jaffe, Susan (1995). Holiday Inn harassers: The case of the abusive guests. *Nation*, April 3, Vol.260, No.3, p. 454.

Strutton, David & Pelton, Lou E. (1995). Sex differences in ingratiatory behavior: An investigation of influence tactics in the salesperson-customer dyad. *Journal of Business Research*, Sept./Oct., Vol.34, No.1, p.35-45.

Discipline

 As many in the service industry believe, customers are always right ... even if they are wrong. Aside from the obvious racist aspects, your co-worker's insult of a customer was unacceptable because it will be reported to other potential customers, who will not patronize your company. You should be concerned about the apparent lack of reaction by management.

For a disciplinary system to work, rules and regulations, a system of progressive penalties, and an appeals process for the employee should be in place. If there is no rule against insulting customers, there should be. It is possible that an oral reprimand was issued to the co-worker, and your work group is unaware of it due to confidentiality. However, at a minimum, she should be transferred out of your work group, or morale will continue to deteriorate.

Your supervisor apparently failed to apply the hot stove rule to the disciplinary process. When someone touches a hot stove, they know they'll get burned and they get burned no matter who they are, every time they touch it. It should be the same way with a violation of company rules and standards. The employees should know they will be disciplined and receive that discipline every time, no matter who they are. In this way, employees are trained to eliminate the undesired behavior. Correction of improper behavior rather than mere punishment is a focus of a positive disciplinary process.

Finally, a lack of racial sensitivity is evident on the part of at least one employee at this work place, and raising consciousness in this area should be an element of correcting this behavior. Perhaps a trained facilitator could meet with the work group so existing resentments can be surfaced, discussed, and resolved. This may aid in restoring morale.

Additional references:

Klaas, Brian S. & Wheeler, Hoyt N. (1990). Managerial decision making about employee discipline: A policy-capturing approach. *Personnel Psychology*, Vol.43, p.117-134.

Ramsey, Robert D. (1998). Guidelines for the progressive discipline of employees. *Supervision*, February, Vol.59, No.2, 1998, p.10-12.

Diversity

 The problem with "Jim" illustrates the difficulties in managing a diverse workforce and in using knowledge, skills, and abilities as the only criteria in making a hiring decision.

Recently, human resource management has focused on hiring applicants who have the knowledge, skills, and abilities required of the task and downplayed the impact of the applicants' demeanor. Knowledge and skills are crucial, of course, but it is also important to consider an applicant's personality and how that person fits in with other members of the work team and with your organization.

You probably have hired other individuals who had excellent qualifications and didn't seem to work well with the team; even the best skills did not overcome rifts that resulted from personality conflicts. Perhaps these individuals were brash Yankees whose attitudes didn't quite mesh with people from your part of the country, or maybe they were members of other sociocultural groups who were in some way different from the bulk of your workforce. Or it's even possible that they were disagreeable, emotionally unstable, closed-minded jerks.

In focusing only on skills and abilities, organizations leave themselves open to challenges when they hire individuals who do not mesh with other members of the workforce. Certain types of people are attracted to certain types of organizations and once selected to work in those organizations will tend to stay and be productive if there is a true match between the applicant and the organization. In hiring individuals from diverse groups, you may get a mismatch sometimes, but you also gain different perspectives and different types of skills. For example, "Jim" may tend to confront a minor problem more directly and get it solved while another manager might want to avoid the problem and let it fester into a blow-up.

The key challenge in managing diversity is establishing an atmosphere that enables all employees to perform up to their potential. By hiring Jim, you are exposing your employees to an individual with a different background and a distinct approach to the job.

Because Jim is a supervisor and does not interact with the hourly employees as equals, he also would benefit from some counseling from you about how these employees may be different from those with whom he worked elsewhere. The bottom line for you is to create an environment in which differences in sex, ethnicity, and culture are identified and acknowledged and do not interfere with the goal of all employees performing at the highest levels possible.

Unfortunately, a sourpuss personality transcends ethnic and cultural differences and might not fit in despite your best efforts at managing a diverse workforce.

Additional references:

Bond, Meg A. & Pyle, Jean L. (1998). The ecology of diversity in organizational settings: Lessons from a case study. *Human Relations*, Vol.51, p.589-623.

Thomas, R. R. (1990). From affirmative action to affirming diversity. *Harvard Business Review*, March/April, Vol.90, No.2, p.107-117.

Drug testing

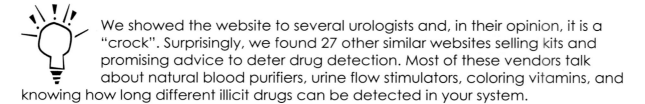 We showed the website to several urologists and, in their opinion, it is a "crock". Surprisingly, we found 27 other similar websites selling kits and promising advice to deter drug detection. Most of these vendors talk about natural blood purifiers, urine flow stimulators, coloring vitamins, and knowing how long different illicit drugs can be detected in your system.

Most drug tests screen for illegal drugs as well as natural substances in the urine that should be present in the sample. If no drugs are detected but natural substances are absent, then the test is noted as positive due to suspected tampering. However, the advertisements are correct in their assertion that job applicants can avoid detection of drug use if they remain drug-free for a sufficient period of time prior to taking a test. The extent to which this type of cheating occurs is not known. But, because of this potential detection problem, some employers have turned to another method of screening, hair follicle testing. A three-inch hair segment will record six months of prior drug use, and if you have a secondary concern regarding rights of privacy, the technique is viewed by most individuals as being less intrusive.

Is the expense and trouble of drug testing worth it? The research evidence suggests it is. According to Bureau of Labor Statistics data, 12 percent of job applicants tested were found to test positive for illegal drugs, with certain industries testing at higher rates than others. For example, 25 percent of individuals who applied for retail positions and were drug tested failed. Further, in one study where testing was conducted, but results were not used in hiring decisions, the applicants who had tested positive were absent 41 percent more often and fired 38 percent more often than those who had not tested positive.

Additional references:

Brady, Teresa (1997). Bad hair days: Hair follicle testing offers an alternative to traditional drug tests. *Management Review*, Vol.86, No.2, p.59-61.

Comer, Debra, R. (2000). Employee's attitude toward fitness-for-duty testing. *Journal of Managerial Issues,* Spring, Vol.12, No.1, p.61-72.

Cranford, Michael (1998). Drug testing and the right to privacy: Arguing the ethics of workplace drug testing. *Journal of Business Ethics*, Vol.17, No.16, p.1805-1815.

E-mail use/abuse

According to the Society for Human Resource Management in Alexandria, Virginia, more than 36 percent of 500 executives who were surveyed reported that they regularly look at e-mail addressed to other employees. In addition, it seems the courts view this snooping as acceptable, even if the employees don't know about it.

Electronic monitoring of this kind is not a particularly new phenomenon in organizations. For example, phone monitoring (or at least the review of phone logs) has been a standard practice for years in many organizations. However, we recommend that organizations have a clear policy regarding e-mail and Internet activity, and that employees be made aware that what is said and done on company time becomes the company's business.

Additional references:

Fusaro, Roberta (1998). Training video tackles e-mail abuse. *Computerworld*, July 20, Vol.32, No.29, p.39.

Petersen, Scot (1999). Is scanning the way to stop employee e-mail abuse? *PC Week*, March 22, Vol.16 p.123.

Sullivan, Eamonn (1998). Be my valentine, but not by corporate e-mail. *PC Week*, February 23, Vol.15, No.8, p.34.

Emotions & expressing opinions in meetings

 Neither perspective is totally correct. You need to give individuals a chance to express their feelings. But you can't get bogged down in directionless emotional confrontation.

Feelings need to be accepted, acknowledged as real, and structured in a way that allows the group to develop and analyze the facts in a more objective way. Don't attempt to bulldoze ahead with the planned agenda and cover up the feelings. Further, no matter how long the meeting, you usually can't overpower an individual with logic if that individual is blocked by emotion.

When things get hot, it's often helpful to take a short break and ask everyone to put their feelings down on paper. This may sound corny, but it is difficult to think clearly about an issue when emotions are running high. Afterward, put the issues on a flip chart and have a discussion in an attempt to get at the facts. Finally, move from getting the facts to finding a solution with which everyone can live, if not totally accept.

Additional references:

Esser, James K. (1998). Alive and well after 25 years: A review of groupthink research. *Organizational Behavior & Human Decision Processes*, Vol.73, p.116-141.

McShulskis, Elaine (1996). Managing employee conflicts. *HR Magazine*, September, Vol.41, No.9, p. 6.

Underwood, J. Chandler (1998). How to manage your anger. *Women in Business*, Jan./Feb., Vol.50, No.1, p. 32-35.

Employment-at-will

He is, for the most part, correct. Your state, Louisiana, is an "employment-at-will" state, and with very few exceptions he can terminate employees without just cause. Employment-at-will is created when an employee agrees to work for an employer but there is no specification of how long the parties expect the agreement to last. This gives workers <u>and</u> employers the ability to terminate the work relationship when either party sees fit to do so. Employers have used this centuries-old common-law rule to assert their right to end the employment relationship at any time for any cause. Although the law was intended to give both the employer and the employee equal footing in the employment relationship, it has become apparent in recent years that employment-at-will has stacked the deck in favor of the employer. Because of the employment-at-will doctrine, many employees who are wrongfully discharged have few legal remedies.

Although employment-at-will is primarily a matter of state law, federal law <u>does limit</u> an employer's right to terminate at-will employees for such reasons as race, age, sex, religion, national origin, union activity, reporting of unsafe working conditions, and disability.

Further, the courts have found that an "implied employment contract" from either terms in an employee handbook or statements made during an employment interview limits the right of employers to discharge. The employer must follow the policy manual or employee handbook's terms and provisions. For example, if you tell a new employee that once she/he has completed a probationary period, the employee can expect to remain with the organization as long as there is satisfactory performance, then you must have just cause for termination. Similarly, if you have a disciplinary system in place yet fail to go through all its steps, you may face a claim of "wrongful discharge."

Several steps should be considered by employers who wish to avoid claims of wrongful discharge:

- Develop clear, objective criteria for evaluating performance.

- Avoid statements when interviewing and recruiting such as "You'll be with us as long as you do your job" or "You will have a long, rewarding, and satisfying career with us."

- Add a statement to the policy manual that the employee handbook is not a contract and that any employee may be terminated at any time for any reason.

Additional references:

Anonymous, (1993). At-will employment. *Employment Relations Today*, Vol.20, No. 3, p.347-350.

Falcone, Paul (1998). Using employment-at-will and probationary periods to withstand termination challenges. *Employment Relations Today*, Summer, Vol.25, No.2, p.75-84.

Hilgert, Raymond (1991). Employers protected by at-will statements, *HRMagazine*, March, Vol.36, No.3,p.57-59

Empowerment

 Evidence indicates that empowered employees are more productive, more satisfied with their jobs, and create higher-quality products than employees who are not empowered. However, for empowerment to work, supervisors such as yourself must give up control and allow the employees to make many decisions, set and accomplish goals, and receive the credit (and blame) for the results. This creates a quandary for you because you believe that, as the supervisor, you should be in charge and do all of the thinking and that others should not get the power and the rewards you deserve by virtue of your position.

Based on your question, it appears your company is not doing a very good job at implementing its empowerment program. Perhaps neither you nor the employees have been prepared properly for a workable transfer of power from the managers to the employees. You describe employees who just want to be told what to do. Have you and others given them a chance to make decisions, to train them to take an active role in setting goals and accomplishing them? Or have you trained them to be told what to do and that you will make all of the tough decisions?

As a supervisor, you don't seem willing to empower your employees because you don't believe they are competent enough and aren't interested in taking on any more responsibility. Other managers might feel they will lose recognition and rewards—and their jobs—if the workers are empowered to make the important decisions while other managers have a high need to control everything going on around them.

The feeling you have that the employees don't want to make decisions can become a self-fulfilling prophecy. If you worked to increase their confidence, you might see more curiosity on their part about getting involved in planning and goal setting. Research indicates that managers should work to instill a sense of personal competence and a sense of personal control in the employees they wish to empower.

In addition, it is important for employees to feel secure in their jobs, to sense that their activities are valued by the company, and to feel that they don't have to be coerced into being involved in work activities. By boosting these key areas among the employees, you may find that your employees have many important contributions to make toward the success of the work unit. But first you must accept the fact that non-supervisory employees do not check their brains at the door each morning.

Additional references:

Hequet, Marc (1995). The new trainer. *Training*, December, Vol.32, No.12, p.23-29.

Markels, Alex (1998). Power to the people. *Fast Company*, Feb.-March,Vol.13, p.154-165

Expatriate manager

Thirty percent of companies expect staff to relocate overseas in the next two years, so you are not alone. In fact, 3.2 million Americans already live in foreign countries. The filling of an international job posting is more complicated, but it follows the same basic procedure as any selection decision. A job analysis is conducted to determine job description and qualifications. Applicants are recruited. The applicant pool is screened via tools such as tests, assessment centers, and background and reference checks, and job interviews are conducted with the best candidates. The company also must plan an orientation and training program to acclimate the manager to a new culture, and you must plan to support that manager in the new position.

Step one then is to determine the duties and qualifications of the successful applicant. This process would follow the standard job analysis you are now using, but it must be modified to meet the needs of the position you are attempting to fill. This requires research into the prospects for your company's line of business in Hong Kong as well as research into the business climate and culture of Hong Kong.

As you put together a job analysis for the position, you may find that the usual skills needed for a domestic position are not the deciding factor when a global posting is considered. Companies often select expatriate managers based upon technical skills, personality, attitudes, and motivation. But technical skills have little, if anything, to do with the employee's ability to adjust to a new environment, to work with foreign colleagues, or to adapt to a foreign culture. Hiring managers generally emphasize perseverance, patience, initiative, flexibility, and a tolerance for ambiguity. Tolerance for ambiguity means the willingness to be exposed to and work well in situations that are hazy and not clear-cut.

In the recruiting process, some organizations use headhunters (executive search firms) to establish an applicant pool. If the use of a search firm exceeds your budget, you may want to place ads in English-language newspapers in Asia such as the *Far Eastern Economic Review,* based in Hong Kong, and the Asian edition of *The Wall Street Journal.* The point is that you need to use recruiting sources beyond the usual outlets.

There are various instruments you can purchase to assess the suitability of candidates for overseas assignments. One example is Prudential Intercultural's Overseas Assignment Inventory (OAI). The OAI purportedly measures 14 factors that are crucial to cross-cultural effectiveness. These include initiative, social adaptability, personal control, tolerance, and risk-taking. The OAI is designed for companies to identify the best candidates for an overseas assignment and to structure training and counseling programs before sending employees overseas. Employees also can use the OAI to determine suitability for international assignments and make good career decisions. Information about the OAI and other Prudential Intercultural programs is available by calling 1-800-356-6834. Be sure to ask for reports that review the reliability and validity of this instrument, or any other, before purchasing it.

Once the selection of the candidate is made, there are a variety of relocation services, such as Prudential, that can assist in preparing the candidate for the position. Individualized briefing programs such as general global awareness, culture and norms of the host country, communication with locals and by long distance to the home office, and doing business in the host country are available. Skill-based programs such as government relations, negotiation, marketing/sales, and human resource development in the host country also are offered. These programs might provide the technical skills that a flexible, patient, tolerant manager might need to succeed.

If your company is anticipating hiring one person or only a few, it would probably be cost effective for you to engage a consultant to help with this process. We would definitely recommend considering a relocation service to aid in training your expatriate manager if these skills are not available in-house.

Additional references:

Selmer, Jan (1998). Which is easier for Western Business expatriates: Adjusting to Hong Kong or the PRC Mainland, *BRC Papers on Cross-Cultural Management,* January, Hong Kong Baptist University.

Teagarden, Mary B. & Gordon, Gary D. (1995). Corporate selection strategies and expatriate manager success. In Selmer, Jan (Ed.*), Expatriate Management: New Ideas for International Business,* Westport, CT: Quorum, p.17-36.

F

Family concerns & questions

The issue of which questions to ask when attempting to fill a position is a tricky one. Many in the human resources field would get very uncomfortable if an interviewer were to ask questions about family, spouse, or even hobbies because these kinds of questions could provide ammunition for an unsuccessful candidate to claim illegal discrimination in the selection process. Often, we hear individuals make the claim that questions such as these are illegal. They are not illegal per se, but they are unwise because they can be used as evidence of discrimination by the company. This is particularly true when organizations are filling positions within the United States. The argument can be made that an applicant's family situation is irrelevant to the success of the applicant in the job. Whether that applicant is up for a post in Lafayette, Louisiana, or Long Island, the applicant's spouse and family situation are said not to matter.

However, when we move to the international scene, information about spouse and family becomes more job-related and therefore more open to inquiries from those who are doing the hiring. Questions about the family are job-related because the assessment of an expatriate manager's family situation appears to be crucial to the success of that manager. Research indicates that when family situation variables are assessed, there is a lower percentage of early returns to the home country, and a higher proportion of expatriates achieve the organization's goals. One of the major reasons why expatriates end assignments early is the inability of the family members to adjust to the host country.

Forty percent of employees who are transferred abroad have spouses who worked before relocating. In some cases, these "trailing spouses," an unfortunate term for people married to expatriates, are prohibited from working in the country where expatriates are assigned, or cannot find work there due to language barriers or economic conditions. In many cases, the culture of the host country is quite different from that of the United States, and it is reasonable to inquire whether the expatriate's family would be able to overcome culture shock. Availability and quality of schools for the expatriate's children are also issues that should be discussed in the selection process. Issues such as these should be explored before a selection is made.

As long ago as 1992, according to *The Wall Street Journal*, American Telephone & Telegraph Co. was asking its candidates for overseas transfers such questions as

- Would your spouse be interrupting a career to accompany you on an overseas assignment? If so, how do you think this will [affect] your relationship with each other?
- How important is it for you to spend significant amounts of time with people of your own ethnic, racial, religious, and national background?
- Has it been your habit to vacation in foreign countries?

Many companies integrate the expatriate's family into training and orientation sessions about the host country before departure. Almost half of the employers who transfer employees abroad provide information or job help to the spouse. These efforts include trying to find a job for the spouse within the company, pressuring the spouse's current employer for a job, or providing leads through customers or suppliers. Companies also have invested in sending the family into the country for a temporary period to determine if family members would be able to adjust to the move. These measures would be a great deal more expensive and impractical to offer to all applicants. Thus, as a screening mechanism, it is a sound, job-related strategy to inquire about the family of an applicant for an international assignment.

We also would question the job irrelevance of family situation to domestic transfers as well. Moving a family and a "trailing" spouse across the country may create problems for the jobholder that would cause that person not to do well in the position. There are different cultures in different parts of the United States, and moving teen-aged children away from their schools and spouses away from their own jobs could create difficulties in job performance. As long as the case can be made that the move would create an adverse impact leading to failure on the job, family issues can be carefully explored. The key is to base any inquiries on job relatedness and ensure that the practical result of these inquiries is not a pattern of discrimination based on race, sex, age, disability, religion, or other categories protected under discrimination laws. If questions such as these are asked, they should be posed to all applicants, not selectively. U.S. companies must obey federal laws concerning discrimination in international as well as domestic operations.

Additional references:

Fitzgerald-Turner, Barbara (1997). Myths of the expatriate life. *HR Magazine*, June, Vol.42, No.6, p. 65-74.

McEvoy, G.M & Parker, B. (2000). The contemporary international assignment: A look at options. In Mendenhall & Oddou, G. (Eds.), *Readings and cases in International Human Resource Management (3rd ed)*, Cincinnati: South-Western, p.470-485.

Fetal protection policy

 Fetal protection policies, such as the one you are considering, gained prominence in the 1980s when Johnson Controls, a battery manufacturer, restricted access by women of childbearing age to jobs involving contact with lead in its company plants. They were concerned about the risk of lawsuits. The union sued for sex discrimination and the Supreme Court ruled against the company, stating that such policies violate Title VII. We recommend that you inform the employees of the risks and let the pregnant employees make their own decisions as to whether alternative work assignments are in order. Of course, this doesn't take you off the hook as far as keeping the work environment as safe as possible. Look for ways to keep such patient incidents from occurring at all. For example, are you adequately staffed to deal with a disruptive patient? Have appropriate measures been taken to ensure both the patient's and the employee's safety, other than restricting access? These are the decisions in which you should be involved. Don't make the decision for the pregnant employees.

Additional references:

Fletcher, Meg (1993). Fetal protection ruling spurs employee education efforts. *Business Insurance*, Dec. 27, Vol.27, No.53, p.2-4.

Guynn, Jessica (1997). California industries struggle with fetal protection rules. *Knight-Ridder/Tribune Business News* (originated from *Contra Costa Times*, Walnut Creek, Calif.), Dec. 7.

Hearit, Keith Michael (1997). On the use of transcendence as an apologia strategy: The case of Johnson Controls and its fetal protection policy. *Public Relations Review*, Fall, Vol.23, No.3, p. 217-231.

FMLA

 First of all, you are not required by federal law to give an employee 12 weeks of unpaid leave because your company is not covered under the Family and Medical Leave Act. The act applies to private businesses of 50 or more employees. Under the Pregnancy Discrimination Act, you are required to provide the same disability income benefits to all employees regardless of pregnancy; thus, you are obligated to provide your employee with the four weeks' paid disability leave.

Now, as to what you should do. If your company can afford it, you might consider providing the employee with an additional eight weeks of leave—unpaid—and using temporary employees to fill in until she returns to work. There are several excellent temporary services that could provide for your needs regarding payroll and other clerical duties until your employee returns. In fact, you could probably get the same person to work for you all 12 weeks if you are satisfied with the job he/she does. We offer this idea because you hold this employee in high regard and would like to keep her on your staff. If you demand that she return to work after a month or quit, she may decide she no longer wants to work with a month-old child in the house, especially for your company. After all, she has done a valuable job for five years and may have been counting on you to help her out in this situation. Thus, playing hardball may lose a good employee.

However, if you take this course of action, you may open yourself up to providing unpaid leave to all of your employees. Although the Family and Medical Leave Act does not apply to your company, it does provide for parental leave for fathers as well as mothers, for personal illness and family illness as well as for the care of an elderly parent. If you decide to provide 12 weeks' leave in this case, even though you are not required to do so, your other employees may expect the same treatment in the future. Thus, the decision boils down to what you believe your company can afford balanced against the morale and retention of your employees. You also may find it useful to establish a company policy on employees who become temporarily unable to work. Take care not to write the policy singling out pregnant employees or you will run afoul of the law.

Additional references:

Anonymous, (1999). Male plaintiff wins FMLA case. *Business Insurance*, Feb. 8. , p.1.

Anonymous, (1999). Questions & answers employees may ask about the FMLA. *Workforce*, January, Vol.78, p.E2-3.

Simerly, Janine S. (1999). What to do after an FMLA leave. *Workforce*, April, Vol.78, p.104-107.

Your Rights
Under The
Family and Medical Leave Act of 1993

FMLA requires covered employers to provide up to 12 weeks of unpaid, job-protected leave to "eligible" employees for certain family and medical reasons.

Employees are eligible if they have worked for a covered employer for at least one year, and for 1,250 hours over the previous 12 months, and if there are at least 50 employees within 75 miles.

Reasons For Taking Leave:

Unpaid leave must be granted for *any* of the following reasons:

- to care for the employee's child after birth, or placement for adoption or foster care;
- to care for the employee's spouse, son or daughter, or parent, who has a serious health condition; or
- for a serious health condition that makes the employee unable to perform the employee's job.

At the employee's or employer's option, certain kinds of *paid* leave may be substituted for unpaid leave.

Advance Notice and Medical Certification:

The employee may be required to provide advance leave notice and medical certification. Taking of leave may be denied if requirements are not met.

- The employee ordinarily must provide 30 days advance notice when the leave is "foreseeable."
- An employer may require medical certification to support a request for leave because of a serious health condition, and may require second or third opinions (at the employer's expense) and a fitness for duty report to return to work.

Job Benefits and Protection:

- For the duration of FMLA leave, the employer must maintain the employee's health coverage under any "group health plan."

- Upon return from FMLA leave, most employees must be restored to their original or equivalent positions with equivalent pay, benefits, and other employment terms.
- The use of FMLA leave cannot result in the loss of any employment benefit that accrued prior to the start of an employee's leave.

Unlawful Acts By Employers:

FMLA makes it unlawful for any employer to:

- interfere with, restrain, or deny the exercise of any right provided under FMLA:
- discharge or discriminate against any person for opposing any practice made unlawful by FMLA or for involvement in any proceeding under or relating to FMLA.

Enforcement:

- The U.S. Department of Labor is authorized to investigate and resolve complaints of violations.
- An eligible employee may bring a civil action against an employer for violations.

FMLA does not affect any Federal or State law prohibiting discrimination, or supersede any State or local law or collective bargaining agreement which provides greater family or medical leave rights.

For Additional Information:

Contact the nearest office of the Wage and Hour Division, listed in most telephone directories under U.S. Government, Department of Labor.

U.S. Department of Labor
Employment Standards Administration
Wage and Hour Division
Washington, D.C. 20210

WH Publication 1420
June 1993

U.S. GOVERNMENT PRINTING OFFICE:1996 171-169

G

Gambling

 Before you completely disregard your fellow manager's concerns, be aware that workplace gambling doesn't always, but certainly can, get out of hand. Besides the NCAA tournaments, you'll find Super Bowl pools, baby pools, fantasy or rotisserie baseball leagues, company lottery ticket purchases (co-workers combining their money when jackpots get large), and even "paycheck poker" with the jackpot going to the employee with the five best numbers in his check serial number. Access to the Internet at work provides employees with further opportunities to gamble online at the comfort of their desks.

A report released in March 1999 by the National Opinion Research Center at the University of Chicago estimated that 5.5 million adults are problem or pathological gamblers and that another 15 million could be at risk of developing gambling problems. Similar to other addictive behaviors, compulsive gambling can bring a host of problems to the workplace, not the least being the appearance that the gambler is being fiscally irresponsible or not tending to business. Recently, one Wall Street investment firm fired four workers in their bond-trading departments for "spending too much time and money" on office pools. One of the four reportedly lost $330,000 during a tournament.

As you noted, office pools also can have a positive effect on the workplace. Your observation echoes the recent results of a national survey on gambling in the workplace administered to human resource managers. Of the respondents who reported knowing that their employees take part in gambling activities, only 6 percent felt gambling had a negative effect on productivity. Thirteen percent felt the activity had a positive impact, while more than half of the respondents felt there was no effect on worker productivity at all.

So, should the pools come to an end? While your company must weigh the benefits against the costs we've enumerated, perhaps the most important consideration is whether such forms of gambling are illegal in your jurisdiction. In many states, the operation of or participation in a gambling pool is a misdemeanor. Although workplace gambling is seldom prosecuted, a manager who selectively enforces laws or company policies sends a dangerous message to employees. In most states, it is legal to conduct and participate in an office pool as long the pool administrator is not running it as a business. In contrast, gambling on the Internet often is illegal. If this is so in your state, you would want to make certain that such activity didn't occur on your premises.

Although many companies have adopted a policy in regard to workplace gambling, such a policy is often viewed as "unduly restrictive," and in turn can have a negative impact on the employees' attitudes toward their work and toward their employer. To prevent this from occurring, if you find a policy is necessary, it is wise to include employees in the process of establishing a new policy. In other words, get input from those who will be governed by the policy. In addition, it is critical to focus on and clearly communicate the legal and/or business justifications for the new policy. Finally, benchmark your policy with others in similar industries and in your market. We're *willing to bet* that you will be pleased with the outcome.

Additional References:

Flanigan, William G. (1997). Everyone into the pool. *Forbes*, Sept., Vol.160, No.5, p.237.

Stuart, Peggy (1991). The hidden addiction. *Personnel Journal*, November, Vol.70, No.11, p.103-108.

Gender & leadership

 One good way to start is to realize that men and women have a tendency to use different leadership and communication styles. Thus, what appears to be conflict in how you do your jobs and how you relate to one another could very well result from the differing approaches each of you takes to your supervisory positions. Research indicates that women tend to use more of a participative style of leadership, seeking to nurture their followers, while men are more likely to use a directive style, seeking to control their followers.

Having said that, we should point out that the most effective managers are able to use either style depending upon the situation they face. In some cases, particularly when employee acceptance of a decision is key, participation is important, and in other instances employees would benefit most from clear direction.

According to research into sex differences in leadership style, women are more likely than men to share power and information and make more of an attempt to improve their employees' self-worth. Women may tend to motivate by convincing followers to think more about the goals of the organization than their own self-interest while men are more likely to hand out rewards for good work and punishment for bad work. The key point to remember is that these are tendencies based on the sex of the leader and not necessarily practiced by all women and all men in managerial positions.   In general, behavior in organizations is determined by a complex interaction between our personality traits and "makeup" and the external environment.

It is important in any job or any situation not to become frustrated with a colleague because she has a different approach than you do to problem solving and leadership. You may be misinterpreting careful consideration of issues for a lack of drive or enthusiasm merely because you have a high level of drive and enthusiasm and a low-key approach is alien to what's normal to you. Possessing insights into differences in leadership and communication styles may form the basis for you to talk to Valerie about the varying ways you approach your jobs. Perhaps if this discussion takes place, you could learn from each other.

Additional References:

Dahle, Cheryl (1998). Women's ways of mentoring. *Fast Company*, September, Vol.17, p.186-195.

Park, Daewoo (1997). Androgynous leadership style: An integration rather than a polarization. *Leadership & Organization Development Journal*, Vol.18, p.166-171.

Gossip

We believe the answer is probably not a training video, and we doubt you will solve the problem by focusing on the employees. You would only be dealing with the symptom of the problem, not the problem itself. A Chinese proverb applies here: "For every 100 men who cut the branches of a diseased tree, only one man inspects the roots." What is the root cause of the gossip and rumors? In our experience, the major reason gossip gets started and has such an impact is because management does such a poor job of communicating. The employees are simply filling the communication void and trying to make sense of a situation to which they are exposed. Get the grapevine working on your side by providing people in your organization with accurate and complete information about what is going on. When you hear a rumor, immediately refute it with indisputable facts and try directing people's attention to other positive things they already believe about the subject of the rumor. For example, do you remember the McDonald's rumor? It was found that reminding people of the positive things they thought about

McDonald's (e.g., cleanliness, family orientation) helped counter the negative effects of the rumor. The one downside of refuting a rumor is that you may actually spread it among those who haven't heard about it. Above all, increase the flow of communication.

Additional References:

Anonymous, (1994). Did you hear it through the grapevine? *Training & Development*, October, Vol.48, No.10, p.20-21.

D' O'Brian, Joseph (1993). Coping with a rumor mill. *Supervisory Management*, Vol.38, No.3, p.6-7.

Group conflict

You've got a great deal of potential for intragroup, as well as intergroup, conflict and a real challenge for a team leader because members of your team are different in the way they regard their jobs; they appear to be in different states of professional consciousness. It's an interesting mix.

First, you are probably a company loyalist, a person who feels very positive about the group and the organization. Your biggest danger may be coming off as so positive that you lose credibility. It is critical that you are on the team because you counterbalance the group cynic, the person who is constantly on the attack. When there is someone like you in the group to keep the cynic under control, the cynic is important because she plays the role of constantly questioning the group's assumptions and challenging it to do better.

The first member of your group, who doesn't care about anything, is a burnout. Burnouts in the group are not going to do much, and they are usually protected if they have worked hard in the past. You must decide whether you and the other team members want the burnout to stay on the team or seek to have him removed.

The young turk is the teammate who is always seeking change. Usually, the turk wants changes that will improve the group and the productivity of its members. The turk has no use for the unproductive burnout and is always going to challenge the fifth member of your group to improve performance. The turk may be in danger of eventually becoming a burnout and of increasing conflict within the team. The fifth member, the old buffalo, provides stability by doing a reliable job and giving the team a sense of history. Old buffaloes are particularly good at orienting new team members.

As team leader, the key is balancing the three potentially productive people with your goals to be an effective team.

Additional References:

Brockmann, Erich (1996). Removing the paradox of conflict from group decisions. *Academy of Management Executive*, May, Vol.10, No.2, p.61-62.

Van Slyke, Erik J. (1997). Facilitating productive conflict. *HR Focus*, April, Vol.74, No.4, p.17.

H

Health inquiries of job applicants

The Americans with Disabilities Act, which now applies to any organization with 15 or more employees, prohibits discrimination against those with disabilities in hiring or promotion. You may ask job applicants if they have any physical or mental condition preventing them from performing the duties of the job for which they are applying, but you may not ask about their disabilities. You may ask applicants about <u>current</u> use of illegal drugs and alcohol. However, if the applicant is a drug addict or an alcoholic and has entered a treatment program, the applicant is considered disabled and questions about the addiction are out of bounds.

A physical examination, at company expense, may be required before a prospective employee starts work. Often, such examinations are performed to determine baseline physical condition to prevent employees with pre-existing conditions from falsely claiming on-the-job injury. Also, pre-employment drug tests can be performed. If you require physical examinations for all prospective employees, you also may require them of individuals with disabilities. You cannot single out applicants with possible disabilities as the only ones requiring physical exams. To protect yourself from legal actions, it is advisable to write job descriptions that detail the duties of each position at your company.

Additional References:

Dickey, Philip L. (1997). The ADA and employment questions: A policy reference guide. *Physician's Management*, June, Vol.37, No.6, p.30-31.

Winans, Brent & Cairns, Gregory (1996). Background checking. *Risk Management*, October, Vol.43, No.10, p. 31-35.

Health plan alternatives

 One way to avoid this problem in the future is to ask the HMO to provide you with an unaltered provider contract, which should specify how the physicians are compensated. If the physicians are "capitated," they receive a set amount, say $30 per month, for each member under their care. If they are "at risk," they lose money if the cost of caring for an HMO enroller exceeds this amount. It is easy to see what will happen to the physician's bottom line if several thousand dollars' worth of expensive tests are ordered and they are capitated with full risk. Physicians who are on salary or who are paid a fee for service have less of a financial incentive to ration health care procedures or make referrals. However, under these latter two methods of compensation, if the average cost of care provided by a physician significantly differs from the HMO's average care costs, the physician's contract may not be renewed.

As for the problems you are currently experiencing, write to the HMO's president, the board of directors, the head of claims, and the head of marketing. Let them know of your concerns as an employer. Help your employees with their appeals by explaining the need for following the HMO's appeal policy to the letter. Suggest that they communicate with the HMO by registered mail and keep copies. Keep records of any problems your employees bring to your attention, and if the problems continue, don't invite the HMO back next year.

Additional References:

Micco, Linda (1998). Americans unsure about type, cost of their health insurance, *HRNews*, June p.14-15.

Shultz, Paul T. & Greenman, Jane F. (1996). Congress advances on health care reform: One step at a time, *Employee Relations Law Journal*, Winter, Vol.22, No.3, p.89-107.

Height & weight inquiries of applicants

 Most companies tend not to make height and weight inquiries because the questions can lead to perceived violations of Title VII and/or ADA. Minimum height restrictions violate Title VII when they disproportionately screen out smaller people in a protected class. This could impact a particular ethnic group or women in general. Placing weight limitations on a position can create problems under ADA, as obesity can be considered a disability under the act.

However, if the employer can prove that the height and weight restrictions are bona fide occupational qualifications (BFOQ) or a business necessity, then it is defensible. For example, if the sales associates in the store are required to wear and model the clothes while functioning as sales reps, the inquiry seems appropriate, particularly if the clothes are sold in a specific range of sizes. Further, it is plausible that there would be a direct relationship between increased sales volume and sales associates wearing the store's clothing line.

Remember, employers can ask any question. However, if they can't demonstrate job relatedness, they will certainly be scrutinized. Perhaps you and your daughter would have seen fewer "red flags" and greater job relatedness if the store had asked an alternative question asking for clothing size.

Additional References:

McShulskis, Elaine (1997). Small business: Be aware of illegal interview questions. *HRMagazine*, June, Vol.42, No.6, p.22.

Bohling, Brinton E. (1998). Employee weight restrictions. *Monthly Labor Review*, March, Vol.121, No.3, P.77-79.

Honesty tests

 Lie detector tests for job applicants are not only questionable, they are illegal in the private sector except when a company is hiring security personnel or employees who will have access to drugs. The abuse of lie detectors and questions about their effectiveness and intrusiveness led to federal restrictions on them in the late 1980s. Lie detectors can be used on employees who are reasonably suspected of involvement in theft from the employer, but there are restrictions and dangers in doing so. It is better to avoid using lie detectors in all but the most extreme cases.

An even more dubious selection tool is graphology, the use of handwriting analysis to infer personality traits. Many U.S. companies continue to use handwriting analysis for certain key jobs. We would advise caution in employing graphology.

This leads to the question of what to do about potentially dishonest employees or job applicants. One might think that the best way to expose a dishonest applicant would be to simply ask blunt questions in an interview (e.g., Have you ever stolen anything from an employer? Have you misrepresented yourself in any way on the application form?). However, because of the face-to-face/social nature of the employment interview, the odds are especially high that the applicant will respond to questions in such a way as to look better to the interviewer. Several studies have found that applicants were more honest in reporting their G.P.A. and SAT scores under nonsocial conditions that involved paper and pencil or computer interviewing as compared to the traditional face-to-face interview. Thus, you should be able to increase the accuracy of information you obtain in the interview by using one of these alternative interview formats.

Many companies, large and small, use such paper and pencil or computer-based psychological honesty tests for job applicants, particularly employees who must handle money and merchandise as part of the job. These pencil-and-paper tests can be purchased from several sources. The tests generally measure attitudes concerning such things as tolerating others who steal and willingness to admit theft-related activities. For example, applicants might be asked whether they would turn in an employee who stole $5 from the company to feed his family and whether they would turn in an employee who stole $100 from the company for the same reason. In both cases, the correct answer is yes, they would turn in the thieving employee, theft being wrong no matter the amount.

However, such tests are not without critics. In some cases, an otherwise excellent applicant is rejected because of a failure to score at a certain level on the test. Whether that employee would have gone on to steal from the company remains an open question. Using honesty tests also raises privacy and ethical questions, and in some states these tests are restricted.

One key with any honesty test is not to use them on a pass–fail basis or as the sole basis for your decision. Checking all references is an important step, including your contacts at a previous company that the employee did not list. Add a clause to your application form that gives you the right to conduct background checks on applicants that include credit checks and motor vehicle reports. (Take care to do this for all applicants and beware that it doesn't result in discrimination against members of protected groups who may be more likely to have poor credit.)

Finally, drug use is often tied to theft. Drug addicts need access to money or merchandise to buy drugs. A pre-employment drug test in combination with establishing a policy that allows the employer to inspect company property such as lockers and desks may be a wise move. The logic behind the policy is that if employees know they will be watched, they will be less likely to engage in dishonest or illegal behavior. Be sure all applicants are given a copy of the policy and they sign a statement that they have read the policy and understand it.

Additional References:

Fletcher, Meg (1997). Making pre-employment screening work: Employers may use background checks, drug tests without running afoul of law. *Business Insurance*, Nov. 10, Vol.31, No.45, p.91.

Leonard, Bill, (1999). Can handwriting analysis help you select and place employees? *HRMagazine*, April, Vol.44, No.4, p.67-73.

Martin, Christopher L. & Nagao, Dennis H. (1989). Some effects of computerized interviewing on job applicant responses, *Journal of Applied Psychology*, Vol. 74, No. 1, p.72-80.

Hygiene

 Although it might be tempting to leave a bar of soap or a stick of deodorant on his desk, we suggest speaking with him directly rather than being so subtle. Jack may have an actual medical problem that causes this difficulty, or he may not pay the same attention to personal hygiene as you and your office mates.

It is important to talk to Jack about personal hygiene because he may not realize that the expectations you and your co-workers have may be different from those to which he is accustomed for whatever reason. Not all cultures disguise or wash away odors as Americans do. Being a little uncomfortable talking about body odor also reflects American culture. Having a chat about it and bringing up the issue of customers and their reactions may be one solution to the problem. It's important to be sensitive because your fellow supervisor may have no idea that others are having a negative reaction to his smell. We often become desensitized to the smell of garlic on our breath from lunch or body odor after a long hot day. Most of us would be slightly embarrassed if it was brought to our attention, but also very appreciative.

As an alternative strategy, you might ask Jack's boss to approach him because the discomfort being felt in the office could be affecting productivity as well as customer service. When the boss becomes involved, the problem is handled no differently than any other situation where an employee falls short of some workplace expectation—be it inappropriate workplace dress or taking too long of a lunch break. If the issue is less one of personal hygiene and actually a medical problem, the boss should encourage Jack to seek the assistance of a dermatologist who will be able to find a way to wipe out the offensive smell.

Your situation brings to mind a lawsuit brought in California against a Citicorp unit several years ago. The plaintiff, a 47-year-old woman, claimed that her offensive body odor was the result of a medical problem and that the company should accommodate her because she suffered from a disability under the Americans with Disabilities Act.

She had no idea she was smelling at all unless someone told her when her intermittent scent erupted. The odor was described as so rancid that one co-worker became physically ill. For a while the woman's boss gently told her when she needed a shower, and some of her colleagues worked out a secret code to let her know when the odor appeared.

However, a new supervisor wanted her to be proactive in preventing the problem from occurring rather than reactive. He reprimanded her repeatedly and sent her home to shower when the smell was noticed.   Simultaneously, the plaintiff began receiving poor job evaluations, partly because of missing work due to being sent home and because of stress-related absences due to the body odor problem. She sued, arguing that the poor evaluations were due to her demands that the company accommodate her disability.

The company argued the plaintiff lacked medical evidence of a disability and that her odor disappeared after she got a warning she would be fired if her hygiene did not improve. After hearing the evidence, the jury deliberated two hours and found in favor of the company.

Additional References:

Anonymous (1994). Offensive body odor may not be a disability. *HR Magazine*, November, Vol.39, No.11, p.12.

Quintanilla, Carl (1998). Oh sure, he's a good job candidate. But how does he smell? *The Wall Street Journal*, June 23, No.124, p.A1(W) p.A1(E) Col.5.

I

Incentives

 Several flaws are apparent in the way the incentive plan was conceived. The owners of the store did not define clear criteria on how the employees would be judged in order to receive the incentive bonus. The program encouraged employees to stock their sections and make them "look nice," and in your view this led some employees to concentrate only on their own part of the store and neglect other important duties such as waiting on customers. No information is provided in the question about how each employee was assigned a section; perhaps the full-timers were given larger sections to handle, and this could have affected their abilities to do well under the incentive program, considering essential tasks that needed to be handled. Failure to make it clear that waiting on customers and answering the phone were important elements of the job may have led the part-time employees to perform in a way that was detrimental to the overall goals of the business.

There are other problems of equity in the incentive program. It is questionable as to whether full-time workers should be compared with part-timers who are only at the store for a limited period of time. The days and times when the part-timers were scheduled to work could have affected the amount of time available to work on the assigned sections. The part-timers (and the owners/managers) also made up a larger voting bloc than the three full-time employees, and this may have hurt the full-time employees' chances to receive the bonus. Majority rule based on vague criteria is a dubious way to distribute rewards, even if it is good enough for the U.S. Congress.

The end result is an incentive program that created unhealthy competition among the small staff and led you and perhaps others to believe the full-timers have little incentive to go beyond the basic duties. Perhaps the owners should write job descriptions that list the employees' essential tasks with an additional task list weighted depending upon the difficulty of each task. Employees who perform the essential tasks competently, as judged by the manager, then might accrue points based on completing the extra tasks. Those who achieved a minimum number of points each week might receive extra compensation. The bottom line is that it is a good idea to tie compensation to performance, but the linkage must be made clear to all employees and fairly designed, or it may create more disincentive than incentive.

Additional References:

Ford, N., Walker, O., and Churchill, G. (1985). Differences in the attractiveness of alternative rewards among industrial salespeople: additional evidence. *Journal of Business Research*, Vol.13, No.2, p.123-138.

Lee, Dong Hwan (1998). The moderating effect of salesperson reward orientation on the relative effectiveness of alternate compensation plans. *Journal of Business Research*, October, Vol.43, No.2, P.65-77

Sanchez, Diane (1999). Putting motivation back in sales incentives. *Sales and Marketing Management*, August, Vol.151, No.3, p.24-26.

Independent contractors

 With great care. The Internal Revenue Service may have a different definition of "employee" than you do, and if so you may pay more to lawyers to fight the IRS than you will save via reclassification of employees as independent contractors. Tax collectors are concerned because independent contractors are not subject to the withholding regulations that apply to employees, and contractors may underreport income.

The September 1994 issue of Inc. magazine offered 20 distinctions between an employee and an independent contractor. Characteristics of employees included workers who are full-time and work for one employer, workers who have a continuing working relationship with an employer and perform duties at the employer's place of business, workers who can be fired by the employer or quit at any time, workers whose duties are essential to the business. If your workers possess these characteristics, they should stay as employees and not be classified as independent contractors.

Another issue to consider is qualification of independent contractors for employee benefits. In a 1996 court case (*Vizcaino v. Microsoft Corp.*), the 9th Circuit ruled that several hundred "freelancers," classified by Microsoft as independent contractors, were really employees who should receive retroactive participation in the company's employee savings and stock purchase plans. The court relied on an earlier IRS determination that the freelancers were employees, rather than independent contractors, for purposes of federal withholding and employment taxes. The court ignored written agreements signed by the freelancers that acknowledged their status as independent contractors responsible for their own taxes, insurance, and other benefits.

Additional References:

Gregory, David L. & Leder, William T. (1996). Employee or independent contractor? Vizcaino v. Microsoft Corporation. *Labor Law Journal*, Vol.47, No.12, p.749-755.

Jenero, Kenneth A. & Mennel, Eric E. (1997). New risks for employers: Misclassified "independent contractors" may be entitled to costly employee benefits. *Employee Relations Law Journal*, Spring, Vol.22, No.4, p.5-24.

Jenero, Kenneth A. & Schreiber, Phillip M. (1998). Drafting effective independent contract agreements. *Employee Relations Law Journal*, Spring Vol.23, No.4, p.127-139.

Internet use/abuse

 The Internet offers employers many benefits, but also raises problems related to productivity, decorum, and employer liability. Using company time to browse the Web, downloading questionable material onto company computers (legally or illegally), and sending e-mail from company accounts to a wide audience are three issues that are troubling many employers like yourself.

If an employee showed pornographic material from the Web to co-workers (e.g., Playboy.com), the *employer* may be subject to a sexual harassment charge of maintaining a hostile work environment.

If information is downloaded illegally or copyrighted material is disseminated without the author's permission, the employer also may be held liable. Further, many hours are spent reading messages from and sending messages to various user groups, and the content of these user group discussions is not always business related. The messages often identify the sender as an employee of a particular company. Most organizations would not want to be identified with their employees' electronic opinions of Bill Clinton, Monica Lewinsky, sexual harassment, and affirmative action.

These concerns have led large companies to set up formal policies regarding employee use of the Internet. You may find it helpful to establish and communicate to employees your company's policy on the use of e-mail and the Web.

While browsing the Web, we came across a summary of the Northern States Power Co. Internet Usage Policy. Its outline can be used to tailor a policy that suits your needs and concerns. The brief summary includes sections on transmittal and receipt of information, accessed information, downloaded software, supervisor monitoring, and auditing of company computers. The auditing function lets employees know that their computer activities will be checked periodically to ensure compliance with the company's policy. Most networking software packages, routing software, and Internet service providers include an auditing function, enabling companies to track website activities.

Employees should understand what you consider an authorized use of the Internet. Still, it is often easy for employees to drift into questionable areas while doing legitimate research.

For example, the Web can be used to get quotes for airline fares. While accessing this information for a future business trip, the employee might want to spend a few more minutes checking fares for an upcoming vacation and a few more minutes accessing restaurant reviews for each city. And while we're at it, how about hotel accommodations and local attractions? And the weather report? And will the basketball team be in town that week? And how have they been doing recently? . . . Of course, employees could do all this over the phone, but links on the Web can generally be made much more quickly and conveniently than repeated phone calls.

As your employees initially explore the Internet, they are learning its capabilities and also becoming more comfortable with the technology. Time spent on surfing is somewhat analogous to the time spent by many employees on game software (e.g., solitaire) loaded on their new computers. After time, the games are seldom played as the novelty wears off. This finding suggests that, similarly, over time, nonbusiness-related surfing also will decline.

Additional References:

Levine, Joshua (1997). The web and the workplace. *Forbes*, June 2, Vol.159, No.11, p.178-180.

Lozier, Katherine R. & Warner, Paul D. (1997). The Internet and Intranet in the workplace. *CPA Journal*, Feb., Vol.67, No.2, p72-75.

Interview questions & sex discrimination

Asking questions that reveal marital status are not illegal per se in most states, but such questions could cause subsequent difficulties if you end up hiring fewer women for these jobs and are faced with a discrimination suit. A question about the marital status of applicants could indicate that you were using the answers obtained to discriminate on the basis of sex.

Your concern about family values may be admirable, but it could result in legal problems for your company. Keep your interview questions narrowly focused on the duties of the job. For example, "Are you willing and able to work long hours, nights, and weekends in this job?" is a much better question than one that inquires about an applicant's marital status.

Additonal References:

Burns Jr., James A. (1993/1994). Implications of the Civil Rights Act of 1991. *Employee Relations Law Journal*, Winter, Vol.19, No.3, p..287-295.

Sack, Steven Mitchell (1998). *The Working Woman's Legal Survival Guide: Know your Workplace Rights Before It's Too Late*. Prentice Hall.

Zigarelli, Michael (1994). *Can they do that?: A guide to your rights on the job*. New York: Lexington Books.

J

Job descriptions

First let's talk about the reasons why your company has job descriptions, and then we'll address the valid points you raise about their usefulness. Job descriptions, which flow from the systematic analysis of jobs within the organization, are quite simply the first line of defense when companies are sued for unlawful discrimination. A proper job description documents the knowledge, skills, abilities, and personality factors that are necessary for the job holder to possess as well as the duties and responsibilities of the employee. Their existence helps to indicate the validity of the company's selection process if challenged in court by showing that the job holder was hired for meeting certain qualifications necessary to job success. The job description also serves as the basis for appraising performance and for compensating employees.

However, as you note, what most organizations are now facing is the prospect of analyzing jobs and writing job descriptions in an increasingly "jobless" world. The movement toward quality, empowerment, and work teams focuses more on the work process and skill sets and less on specialized jobs. Activities at work are steadily changing, new approaches and tasks appear constantly, and the job description is seen by its critics as too static. Good old-fashioned job descriptions restrict employees and encourage them not to perform certain duties and not to stray from a narrow focus. Ten years ago, management guru Tom Peters argued for the elimination of job descriptions: "Perhaps a case could be made for job descriptions in a stable, predictable, very vertically oriented organization. Today, in all cases the 'j. d.' is a loser… It is imperative today that managers and non-managers be induced to cross 'uncrossable' boundaries as a matter of course, day after day." Peters suggested that great coaching serve as an alternative to formal job descriptions.

A company that successfully dumped job descriptions is W.L. Gore and Associates, maker of Gore-Tex waterproof fabrics and employer of more than 5,000 people. Gore has three job titles within the organization (president, secretary-treasurer, and associate), and the first two are required by law to incorporate the business. Gore looks for flexible, adaptable, innovative associates who are expected to fit in where they believe they can make the most valuable contribution to the team. A company mentoring program allows senior associates to help newcomers thrive in the organization. Of course, this approach requires an associate whose personal temperament welcomes constant change and ambiguity. It is also accompanied by a strong culture that stresses fairness, commitment, freedom to grow and develop, and consultation with others on major decisions.

Is the job description a dinosaur? In an organization that focuses on process, successfully changes its culture so as to instill shared values such as those of W.L. Gore, and avoids even the appearance of illegal discrimination, perhaps job descriptions should become extinct. Yet, even if the job descriptions are eliminated, records of the knowledge, skills, abilities, and personal temperament factors needed for employees to succeed no matter what their job or job title should be on file because we live in a lawsuit-happy world. What you look for when you hire employees or associates should be very clearly stated so you can defend yourself in court if necessary.

Additional References:

Bridges, William (1995). A nation of owners: job skills. *Inc.*, May 16, Vol.17, No.7, p.89-92.

Mello, Jeffery (1993). Employing and accommodating workers with disabilities: Mandates and guidelines for labor relations. *Labor Law Journal*, March, Vol.44, No.3, p.162-170.

Nelson, Bob (1999). Seeing the big picture. *Philadelphia Business Journal*, Nov. 26, Vol.18, No.42, p.18.

Job hopping

 In a way, both of you are correct. Job hopping every couple of years can be a red flag indicating an employee who can't be satisfied, has poor work habits, or is unable to work with others. You are correct that past behavior is a good predictor of future behavior, so you can't count on the job hopper to make your company his or her final stop if that is what you are seeking. However, as your friend pointed out, a pattern of job hopping also can be a sign that the person brings a wealth of skills, knowledge, and experience to the job.

We take issue with your friend on his point that loyalty doesn't count for anything. Turnover costs of a good employee are an expensive proposition for an organization to bear. For example, the costs of recruiting, hiring, and getting a manager "up to speed" have been estimated as high as 50 percent of a first-year salary. Frequent employee turnover can play havoc with institutional memory. (Institutional memory refers to the knowledge those with long tenure possess on such details as client likes and dislikes, or even mistakes that have been made that would be costly to repeat.) Finally, organizational commitment tends to be associated with lower levels of absenteeism and a greater willingness to make sacrifices and to go well beyond the job description.

Certainly, going to work for a company after graduation and having the same company give you a retirement watch is no longer the norm, and the reality is that the number of job changes an individual makes over a 10-year period is on the rise. This increase has been attributed in part to the continued corporate downsizings that have prompted individuals to leave before being asked to leave. Downsized and de-layered companies also have taken away opportunities for upward mobility for those who have desired it. Additionally, most employers no longer support the retirement packages of the past that have financially tied employees into their organization, and have instead opted for portable plans and immediate vesting. Further, basic supply-and-demand issues in certain industries have been associated with varied frequencies of job change. As demand increases, recruiters become more aggressive and the offers become more attractive. Even demographic and societal changes have been linked to increased job hopping. Generation Xers, the approximately 40 million Americans born between 1965 and 1976, have been characterized as difficult to retain, valuing company loyalty less than they do interesting work assignments and seeking frequent recognition.

With all this said, recently surveyed executives of the nation's largest 1,000 companies responded that applicants who had held more than five jobs in 10 years would be viewed in a negative light. Industries such as those focused on information technology were a little more forgiving. Perhaps they were more concerned with the cutting-edge technical skills an employee in this industry needs today and the potential for that knowledge to be obsolete tomorrow. Yet even within this low-tenure industry group, the culture and goals of a specific organization may be a more critical factor for determining how many job changes are too many. For example, Intel states, as core to its philosophy, that it is "… committed to having employees develop a sense of ownership about their jobs." As such, it invests $120 million annually on employee training. Clearly then, Intel's goals are not compatible with short-term employment.

Thus, we suggest that a decision as to whether an individual has changed jobs too many times over a period of time take into consideration the norm for your particular industry, the type of position you are filling, the goals and culture of your organization, as well as the pattern of positions and career goals of the individual in question. If a person is changing jobs without progression, it may be that the person is simply moving for more money. An offer higher than the individual's next raise may be too attractive for this individual to resist. On the other hand we know a young accountant who has hopped several times because she was unable to get the diversity of experiences in one firm that would enable her to reach the positions of leadership she desires.

So, ask questions of yourself and the applicant before you make a judgment as to how many moves are too many.

Additional References:

Blumfield, M., Gorden, J., Picard, M., & Stamps, D. (1997). The new job mobility. *Training*, Vol.34, No.5, p.12-14.

Fafard, L. (1998). Career counselor: Job hopping — out of the frying pan, into the fire. *Computerworld*, Sept.14, Vol.32, No.37, p. 20-21.

Jokes & humor at work

 You're only paranoid if they're not after you! Seriously though, if the jokes are directed toward you, banning them would probably just make matters much worse. A recurrent theme in the research on workplace humor is that such oppositional joking constitutes a nonthreatening way for subordinates to "let off steam" and should be encouraged by managers so as to defuse workplace tension and conflict. Don't ignore the joking. Humor consultants (yes, there are such consultants) contend that a humorous managerial response to employee joking implies that those in authority are strong enough to tolerate criticism and admit that mistakes can be made by everyone. Consequently, the rebellion turns into a twisted form of loyalty directed toward the boss.

Of course, "Dilbert" cartoons and paraphernalia may be in your office simply because it hits the funny-bone rather than a nerve. There may be no sinister undertones directed toward you or the company. However, such humor can be a relatively effective means of expressing employee dissatisfaction, especially where more overt forms of resistance, such as restricting output, dissent, defiance, or insubordination, may provoke disciplinary action or even termination. Therefore, you need to make sure that the lines of communication are always open and attempt to get an accurate picture of your employees' frustrations and levels of satisfaction. One systematic way of doing this is through the administration of an annual employee attitude survey. There are quite a few relatively inexpensive, well-designed surveys available with job and industry benchmarks that enable a comparison of your employees' satisfaction levels with employees in similar jobs.

Is there any joking in the workplace that might justify the cartoon ban you propose? Our answer is yes. When the joking takes on a sexual or a racial tone or is generally demeaning, you are obligated to order such a ban so that, among other reasons, the company stays out of the courts. We also feel jokes directed toward the customer also should be banned. We are referring to such posts as "You want it WHEN?" Even if these jokes are not visible to the customer, their presence suggests an attitude inappropriate in an organization that wants to retain its customers.

By the way, you are apparently not the only boss or company that is tired of the "Dilbert" humor. On the Dilbert Zone Financial page of United Media's website, you will find the "Pointy Haired Boss Index." This index tracks the stocks of the publicly traded companies that reportedly block employee access to "Dilbert" on the Internet. At last glance, they weren't faring too well.

Additional References:

http://www.unitedmedia.com/comics/dilbert/financial/tphbx.html

Weise, W.H. (1997). Humor on the job, *Supervision*, November, Vol.58, No.11, p.9-11.

Wynter, Leon E., (1998). What isn't so funny about ethnic jokes, *The Wall Street Journal*, Feb. 4, p.B1(W) p.B1(E) col. 1.

K

Key job responsibilities

 When it comes to the question of "Who is to do what, with what kind of involvement by others?", one useful technique is called key responsibility charting. The first step is to construct a grid; the major types of decisions and classes of actions made by the work group are listed along the left-hand side of the grid, and the individuals who might play some part in decision making on those issues are identified on the top of the grid. Each decision or action is discussed and "key" responsibility is assigned. Discussion then focuses on who has approval–veto power, who provides support, who must be informed but, by inference, cannot influence; and, finally, who does not need to be involved.

This process is not quite as easy as it appears. For example, a person may want approval–veto responsibility on an item but really not need it; a person may not want support responsibility on an item but should have it; or two people may each want key responsibility on a particular item but only one can have it.

Responsibility charting sessions can quickly identify who is to do what on new decisions as well as help to pinpoint reasons why old decisions are not being accomplished as planned.

Additional References:

Coram, Harold F. (1987). Linear responsibility charting. *Management Quarterly*, Fall, Vol.28, No.3, p34-38.

Trey, Beulah (1996). Managing interdependence on the unit. *Health Care Management Review*, Summer, Vol.21, No.3, p.72-82.

Kidnapping, terrorism, & security while abroad

 Kidnapping executives is not just for terrorists any more. Seizing businesspeople and extorting their companies for ransom has become a cottage industry in some countries, and there have been some scary examples in recent years. However, the risk that your managers will be kidnapped or attacked in a foreign country is extremely low. The chances of dying from a dog bite, of being killed by lightning, or of drowning in your own bathtub are greater than being killed by terrorists or kidnappers.

The targets of kidnappers in foreign countries are usually local businesspeople, not foreign visitors. However, it is wise to take security precautions or at least make a risk assessment of the countries you plan to visit. Keeping a low profile, registering with U.S. consulates, staying out of bad areas, and not advertising yourself as an American are sensible precautions that may provide peace of mind and lessen your stress level. After all, 10,000 Americans die overseas every year from natural causes such as heart attacks.

In terms of assessing risk, you should consider the nature of your managers (are they well known or in high-profile jobs?) and the nature of the destination. For example, criminal activity is prominent in Rio de Janeiro, kidnapping is a problem in Mexico and Colombia, robbery is relatively frequent in several Eastern European countries and elsewhere. Once these risks are estimated, your managers should be provided with a summary of the local situation and precaution strategies. In some locations, it might be wise to engage security assistance.

You can get more information about the potential risks and sources of help from the State Department's Bureau of Consular Affairs in Washington, D.C. Information about the Overseas Security Advisory Council, a group whose principal aim is to share facts between government and business, can be obtained from the State Department's Bureau of Public Affairs. Several organizations operate websites where more information can be obtained about international travel risks and sources of security help.

Jules Kroll, a business intelligence firm, recently published a list of the 10 most dangerous cities for business travel. Unfortunately, 4 of those 10 cities are in South America. The top ten list: (1) Algiers, Algeria; (2) Bogotá, Colombia; (3) Caracas, Venezuela; (4) Johannesburg, South Africa; (5) Karachi, Pakistan; (6) Lagos, Nigeria; (7) Medelin, Colombia; (8) Mexico City; (9) Moscow; (10) Rio de Janeiro, Brazil. Don't fear too much: The most dangerous part of an overseas trip remains the drive from your home to the airport.

Additional References:

Commerce Clearing House (1992). 1992 SHRM CCH Survey: International assignments required more personal and family support than what is being provided now. *Human Resources Management*, p.1-12.

Solomon, Charlene (1997). Global business under siege. *Workforce*, Supplement: *Global Workforce*, January, p.18-23.

L

Language restrictions

You can have such a policy, but it should be very narrowly defined and related only to the operations of the business. For example, some companies have policies restricting their employees from speaking anything other than English while at work, and these companies have found themselves in hot water. The U.S. Equal Employment Opportunity Commission views language as a crucial part of a person's nationality and has sued companies charging that strict English-only language policies violate the federal ban on discrimination based on national origin.

Employers can require that their workers be able to speak English and use English in dealing with customers and co-workers who speak only English. In other words, any restrictions must be necessary to the operation of the business. You may want to consider such a policy, particularly because some of your customers have complained. But you can run afoul of the law if you try to stop the employees from speaking a second language in casual conversation, even if co-workers can overhear their remarks.

The *New York Times* has reported that some companies have ordered employees to speak only English when they are in the employee lounge, the restroom, or even while walking outside the company offices. This is a particularly sensitive issue in states with large Hispanic populations such as New York, Florida, and Texas. A group in South Florida called the Spanish American League Against Discrimination told the *New York Times* that about 50 Spanish speakers call each month claiming language discrimination in the workplace. Speakers of other languages such as Vietnamese,

Chinese, Tagalog (a native language of the Philippines), and French Creole also have been targeted by employers at banks, manufacturing plants, department stores, schools, and post offices.

In many instances, the ability to speak a second language adds value to the employee because the employee can converse with diverse groups of customers who have limited knowledge of English. One solution is for you and your employees to learn some Spanish. Then you would know what those two are talking about, and you could respond appropriately! Comprende?

Additional References:

Brady, Teresa (1996). The downside of diversity. *HR Focus*, August, Vol.73, No.8, p. 22.

Cameron, Christopher David Ruiz (1997). How the Garcia cousins lost their accents: Understanding the language of Title VII decisions approving English-only rules as the product of racial dualism, Latino invisibility, and legal in determinancy. *California Law Review*, Vol.85, No.5, p.261-307

Coolidge, Shelley Donald (1998). On the job, it's English or pink slip. *Christian Science Monitor*, January 15, Vol.90, No.35, p.1.

Leadership style

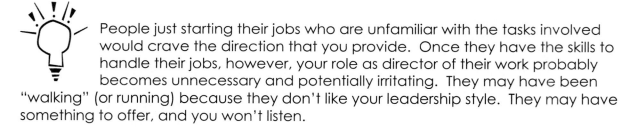 People just starting their jobs who are unfamiliar with the tasks involved would crave the direction that you provide. Once they have the skills to handle their jobs, however, your role as director of their work probably becomes unnecessary and potentially irritating. They may have been "walking" (or running) because they don't like your leadership style. They may have something to offer, and you won't listen.

Participative management cannot be imposed from above. In order to effectively participate in important decisions, employees need to have the skills to perform their jobs, enough information about the issue to help them be effective participants, and supervisors who will take their concerns seriously and respond to them.

Often the effectiveness of leadership style can be influenced by the characteristics of the subordinates, the nature of the tasks they are performing, and the nature of the work unit and the organization. If many of the duties performed by your employees are structured, routine tasks that give them immediate feedback, these jobs would tend to negate your ability to direct work once the employees are properly trained.

Research indicates that managers have difficulty attempting to *direct* the work of experienced professionals. The experience of these individuals and their professional orientation would tend to substitute for the manager's efforts to tell them what to do; it would be wise for managers to allow them a great deal of latitude. The standards of the profession would tend to govern their activities.

With members of a highly cohesive work group, the impact of the manager is decreased because employees like each other and are tightly bonded to one another. In addition, managers who work in organizations that have many policies, procedures, and rules also can see their leadership influence diminished because employees have been trained and rewarded for following standard operating procedure rather than the directions of the manager.

The key to leadership style is flexibility. A capable manager should practice different styles depending upon the characteristics of the employees, the tasks, and the organization.

Additional References:

Heskett, James L. & Schlesinger, Leonard A. (1997). Leading the high-capability organization: Challenges for the twenty-first century. *Human Resource Management*, Vol.36, p.105-113.

Pascale, Richard (1998). Grassroots leadership. *Fast Company*, April-May ,Vol.14, p. 110-120.

Learning organization

 Establishing the ability to become a learning organization may be essential to the future vitality of your company, but roadblocks such as you describe are not unusual. Peter Senge, in his book *The Fifth Discipline*, discusses how "learning disabilities" can be fatal to organizations. He argues that only companies that discover how to be learners will succeed in the rapidly changing global marketplace.

Senge uses the parable of the boiled frog to describe what can happen to organizations that fail to learn. If a frog is put into boiling water, it will immediately jump out to safety. However, if a frog is placed in cool water and the heat is slowly turned up on the water, the frog will just sit there and boil to death. The same is true of organizations. Organizations quickly respond to crisis but will not notice gradual changes in the environment that erode their competitive position.

Learning organizations attempt to amplify weak, subtle cues and attempt to study gradual processes so as to learn from them and anticipate change accordingly. There are five disciplines (hence the book's title) that are required for a learning organization, and the fifth of these, systems thinking, is usually the most important for learning to take place. Systems thinking involves seeing the organization as an interdependent system where what occurs in one part of the system will be felt in varying degrees in the other parts. Systems thinking recognizes that the problems faced today by the organization result from yesterday's solutions, behavior often gets better before it gets worse, and the cure can be worse than the disease. Other requirements of a learning organization include the desire of individuals in the organization to learn and grow, active reflection on the underlying assumptions that guide the actions of managers, and a commitment to team learning.

But the major hurdle your organization appears to face is the lack of a shared vision. Senge sees a shared vision as a force or sense of purpose that provides energy and focus for learning. A shared vision is important because it may be a first step for people who mistrusted each other to start working as a team. Without a shared vision pulling the team toward its goals, the status quo will prevail. It appears that the boss in your organization exemplifies the difference between espoused theories and theories in use. Senge notes that often managers tell people they want to do something or say they view the world in a certain way (an espoused theory), but their actions reveal otherwise (they operate under their theory in use). It is hard to bring up these discrepancies because many of us in organizations practice defensive routines, attempting to avoid conflict while projecting the image that we are competent and know the right answers.

We would suggest keeping up your efforts to be innovative and institutionalize learning within the organization. Meanwhile, sitting down with the boss to discuss the elements of what it takes to be a learning organization would be a good idea. All of you may benefit from taking a look at suggestions included in *The Fifth Discipline*.

Additional References:

Dorsey, David (1998). The new spirit of work. *Fast Company*, Vol.16, August, p.124-134.

Garvin, David (1993). Building a learning organization. *Harvard Business Review*, July-August, p.78-91.

Senge, Peter M. (1990). *The fifth discipline: The art and practice of the learning organization*. New York: Doubleday.

M

Micro-management

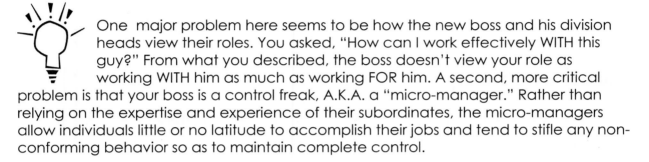 One major problem here seems to be how the new boss and his division heads view their roles. You asked, "How can I work effectively WITH this guy?" From what you described, the boss doesn't view your role as working WITH him as much as working FOR him. A second, more critical problem is that your boss is a control freak, A.K.A. a "micro-manager." Rather than relying on the expertise and experience of their subordinates, the micro-managers allow individuals little or no latitude to accomplish their jobs and tend to stifle any non-conforming behavior so as to maintain complete control.

Usually, micro-managers micro-manage because they are intimidated by new ways of doing things. Change, challenge, empowerment, diversity, and new ideas represent a system out of control to micro-managers. They rely heavily on rules, standard operating procedure, and their organizational position to keep order. Micro-managers may function well in traditional bureaucratic organizations and very stable environments. Unfortunately, they function poorly in the highly competitive and volatile environments where most of us work. Micro-management is also a problem in small mom & pop firms when sudden growth is experienced. It is often difficult for the small business owner to let go of the reins as the company grows. If this doesn't happen, either the growth will stagnate or the small business owner will end up in a coronary care unit.

Given that your other three bosses were leaders who empowered you rather than micro-managed you, and that they succeeded in your organization, we would imagine your new boss and his style will not be as successful. If he doesn't adjust, his tenure with your organization will no doubt be short lived.

Additional References:

Marino, Sal F. (1998) Micromanagement leads to mismanagement. *Industry Week*, July, Vol.247, No.14, p.22.

Pat Wiesner (1994). The sin of micro-management. *Colorado Business Magazine*, July, Vol.21, No.7, p.8.

Military leave

 Yes, you are at risk if you let him go regardless of whether he tells you of a Reserve commitment before hire. Few employers are aware that reservists are protected from such termination and hiring decisions under the Uniformed Service Employment/Re-employment Act. Numerous free publications on the specific responsibilities of employers may be obtained from the Ombudsman section of the Guard and Reserve by calling 1-800-336-4590.

Additional Reference:

Holzinger, Albert G. (1997). When workers are good soldiers. *Nation's Business*. February, Vol.85, No.2, p.50-52.

Money as a motivator

 It's critical to remember that most people, other than Ebenezer Scrooge, value money for what they can obtain with it, not just because they want to hoard it. In addition, many employees see an increase in pay and benefits as a sign that their status is on the rise and they are valued contributors. Other factors are also important in motivating employees, such as improved communication, allowing employees more latitude in making decisions in matters that affect them, providing stimulating work, and establishing job security. These ingredients can play important roles in employee motivation, but they have not displaced pay as the most important motivator in today's organizations. Organizations should use a combination of financial and nonfinancial factors to retain and motivate the work force.

This question raises another issue: the value of management surveys that are reported in newspapers and magazines. Readers should be critical consumers of information— including that presented in this book. Surveys reported in the newspaper should be judged similarly to reports of new medical cures: with healthy skepticism and not as gospel. In particular, readers should inquire about whether a survey's results are statistically significant (could they have occurred by chance?), what methods were used to gather the information (experiment, confidential questionnaires, interviews, etc.), and who funded the study (do they have an interest in finding certain results?).

One recent survey that downgraded the importance of money in relation to other factors such as quality of work life was sponsored by an organization funded by 15 of the nation's largest corporations and foundations. The survey was based on "in-depth interviews with a nationally representative group of 3,400 workers." To evaluate the findings of this study, think how you would respond if someone asked you in an interview why you took your most recent job and what you would define as success at work. Would pay top your list? Perhaps, but if you want to put yourself in a favorable light with the interviewer, you might choose responses that relate more to the nature of the work and quality of life, and less to personal, material benefits.

Additional References:

Grensing, L. (1983). Motivating without money – easier than it seems. *Supervision*, November, Vol.45, p.3-4.

Gupta, Nina, & Shaw, Jason D. (1998). Let the evidence speak: Financial incentives are effective!! *Compensation and Benefits Review*, March-April, p.26, 28-32.

Herzberg, F. (1987). One more time: How do you motivate employees? *Harvard Business Review*, Sept.-Oct., Vol.65, p.109-120.

N

Napping at work

 The organization does have a right to control what occurs on its premises— even during breaks. However, if the employee is in the break room during breaks and comes back to work in the allotted time, there shouldn't be a problem. If the employee is taking extended breaks, then he should be counseled about the tardiness, and it should be treated as an individual performance problem. Some companies do have rules that strictly prohibit sleeping while at work. In such rare cases, the rule is in place to make certain that all employees are alert in the event of an emergency. In your case, it is possible that allowing the naps may help the company avoid a workers' compensation claim of stress and eye irritation as a result of working in the poor air quality of the shop. It sounds like your employee is using *his* time wisely.

Additional References:

Joinson, Carla (1999). Don't forget your shift workers. *HRMagazine*, February, Vol.44, No.2, p.80-84.

Moore, Richard W. (1996). Variety of sleep disorders take their toll on U.S. businesses. *Business Journal-Portland*, September 13, Vol.13, No.29, p.12B-13.

Overman, Stephenie (1999). Rise and sigh. *HR Magazine*, May, Vol.44, No.5, p68-73.

Natural attrition

 Although "the numbers" may ultimately drive whether your organization stays in business, what you've described suggests that too much emphasis is being placed by your CEO on short-term profits rather than on the organization's long-term success. Imagine a batter at home plate concentrating on his batting average rather than his swing. He's thinking about the right thing at the wrong time.

Focusing on short-term profits gives the illusion of control, but it doesn't necessarily inform action in constructive ways. For example, a major aerospace contractor laid off a large number of its experienced engineers in order to meet targeted financial objectives. Though an improved economy was on the horizon, management felt it was important to keep its promises to shareholders in its annual projections. A year later the firm lost several major contracts because it didn't have enough qualified engineers to do the work and couldn't recruit engineers back when the job market got tight.

The rigid implementation of unrealistic budgeting processes, based on short-term financial objectives, can do more to sabotage a company's well-being than almost any other aspect of organizational life. The answer is to develop financial and reward systems that focus on long-term growth and health of the company, not just today's profits. If you think about it, a "Going Out of Business Sale" can be a very profitable last few days for an organization.

Your CEO is correct that many companies are looking for better ways of doing more with fewer people. However, downsizing as well as growth must be part of a well-designed plan with well-understood, long-range goals. For instance, among the products and services your organization provides, which is forecasted for lower demand? Where is growth anticipated? Utilizing natural attrition as a downsizing strategy may leave you overstaffed in an area where demand is low and understaffed in areas where growth is either forecast or desired.

We suggest you discuss with your CEO several alternative ways of measuring success in your company, besides short-term profit. You noted that customers have recently reacted negatively about the quality of what they are provided. Make certain that the CEO is made aware of this information. Finally, make certain that you and the CEO have the same picture in your minds of what the organization will look like three-to-five years from now. A discrepancy between your vision of the organization's future and his vision of the future may explain a lot.

Additional References:

Kerr, Stephen (1995). On the folly of rewarding A, while hoping for B. *Academy of Management Executive*, February, Vol.9, No.1,p.7-14.

Light, David A. (1998). Performance Management: Investors' balanced scorecards. *Harvard Business Review*, Nov.-Dec., Vol.76, No.6, p.17.

Nosy boss

 Fred's discussions with problem employees could cause problems for you because he is apparently focusing his attention not on performance and productivity but on personal issues. These may be more related than you think. However, of greater issue is violating the employees' trust and, at least in some instances, engaging in gossip. Those who are the focus of this gossip may see performance adversely affected. Also, if false information is circulated and repeated, you and Fred could be sued for slander.

To deal with the employees' personal problems, you may want to consider establishing an employee assistance program (EAP) at your company. The Bureau of National Affairs estimates that the cost of an EAP ranges from $12 to $35 per employee each year. EAPs use counseling rather than discipline to aid employees whose personal difficulties may be interfering with their job performance. They focus on identifying the real problem the employee is facing and referring that employee to the appropriate place to get help.

We don't mean to suggest that supervisors have no business probing into personal and private aspects of an employee's life if it is relevant to the job and if the information remains confidential. The supervisor has a legitimate interest in anything that causes performance problems at work, and often has more control over turning things around than is thought.

Additional References:

Bahls, Jane Easter (1999). Handle with care. *HRMagazine*, March, Vol.44, No.3, p.60-64.

Caldwell, B. (1994). EAPs: Survey identifies uses and administration. *Employee Benefits Plan Review*, Vol.9, p. 36-38.

Lucia, Alexander (1997). Leaders know how to listen. *HR Focus*, April, Vol.74, No.4, p.25.

-- **O** --

Off-duty conduct

Many companies have adopted policies that attempt to regulate the off-duty activities of their employees, including their off-duty personal relationships, lifestyle choices, and "moonlighting." In response, many states have enacted legislation intended to protect the lawful off-duty behavior of employees, beyond what the federal laws address. Your state, Louisiana, is not one with such legislation and your boss would probably be on firm ground if he chose to terminate a moonlighting employee. However, regardless of the law, it is, simply stated, a stupid management practice for employers to attempt to regulate off-duty activities of its employees unless the behavior has an adverse effect on job performance or the organization.

We believe that you are correct in your assumption that your employee's commitment to the organization and overall job satisfaction will drop when he is informed of the boss's policy. The ban on "moonlighting" itself may be a factor in this drop. However, the employees' job satisfaction and commitment levels will be likely more affected by the seemingly arbitrary nature of your boss's decision and the lack of justification he has provided. Therefore, you need to have a discussion with your boss as to why he is taking this stand. It may be the case that as the boss discusses his rationale with you, he realizes that he's made a mistake and reverses his position. If not, understanding his perspective may help to lessen the effect of the bad news you'll be giving your employee.

For example, management has a legitimate concern to prevent conflicts of interest a second job may bring, particularly if the second job is helping a competitor or someone who does business with the organization. However, this doesn't seem to be the case in your situation. Further, because your employee is a model performer, the most frequent concern of managers, lowered performance, also seems not to be the case (i.e., the employee will be too tired from working long hours to do a safe or productive job). Management may be concerned that a second job could interfere with the employer's ability to schedule work when needed or conflict with your employee's availability to work overtime. Of course, family commitments, educational commitments, or anything else going on in an individual's life could create the same dilemma.

Finally, if the boss still feels strongly about moonlighting, write a policy statement so that everyone knows up-front why anything that interferes with work performance or required work hours is a legitimate concern of your company.

Additional References:

Samborn, Randall (1994). Love becomes a labor law issue; Wal-Mart firings raise issue of privacy. *The National Law Journal*, Feb. 14, Vol.16, No.24, p.1, col2.

Webster, George D. (1992). Regulating employees' off-duty conduct. *Association Management*, July, Vol.44, No.7, p.99-100.

Older workers

 Many companies stereotype the capabilities of older workers, seeing them as less energetic, as a greater health and safety risk, or as less flexible and technologically adept when compared to younger employees. Some of these stereotypes include grains of truth. For example, studies by the Bureau of Labor Statistics show that workers 55 and older are more than twice as likely as younger workers to die of job-related injuries. However, generalizations about individuals based on perceived or actual characteristics of the groups to which they belong can lead to poor choices in terms of promotion and staffing, including buyouts of older workers and involuntary terminations. In addition, adverse employment actions involving older workers can result in legal action because workers age 40 and older are covered by federal discrimination laws.

On a practical matter, it is important for organizations to consider the changing demographics of the workforce and to make hiring and promotion decisions accordingly. Hiring and retaining older, experienced workers should be a key human resource management strategy at any company. A few statistics may provide a convincing argument: (1) In 2005, the average age of the work force will increase to 40, (2) the number of people age 50 to 65 is increasing at more than twice the rate of the overall population, (3) the number of younger workers will drop from 24 percent of the workforce in 1975 to 16 percent in 2005.

Therefore, it's clear that the shortage of younger workers will worsen, and companies would be wise to retain and promote people in your employee's age group who have the kinds of skills and experience that fit with company goals. Retaining the older worker helps companies lower costs of turnover and training and capitalize on experience offered by these employees. Many companies already have strategies to take advantage of the older worker's experience. These include redeploying older workers onto project teams, establishing a job bank to find retirees to work part time, and using flextime, job sharing, and other methods to retain experienced people.

You may be interested to learn that older employees perform just as well or better than younger employees in jobs not requiring heavy physical labor. They tend to be more patient with customers and may be more trustworthy, knowledgeable, and loyal than their younger counterparts. Finally, they are less likely to job hop—unless, of course, they are denied a promotion for which they are the best qualified candidate.

Additional References:

Carson, Kerry D. & Carson, Paula Phillips (1997). Career entrenchment: A quiet march toward occupational death? *The Academy of Management Executive*, Vol.11, No.1, p.62-75.

Stalnaker, C. Keith (1998). Safety of older workers in the 21st century. *Professional Safety*, June, Vol.43, No.6, p.28-31.

Steinhauser, Sheldon (1998). Age bias: Is your corporate culture in need of an overhaul? *HRMagazine*, July, Vol.43, No.8, p. 86-91.

Sullivan, Sherry E. & Duplaga, Edward A. (1997). Recruiting and retaining older workers for the new millennium. *Business Horizons*, November/December, Vol.40, No.6, p.65-69.

OSHA audits

 Taking employee safety seriously is important for all organizations. Common law requires that employees be provided with safe working conditions, and the Occupational Safety and Health Administration is an agency that was set up by statute to enforce federal workplace safety laws. It writes regulations related to health and safety in the workplace. Also, state OSHA offices conduct workplace safety inspections.

However, there is only a slim chance that an OSHA inspector will visit your company because OSHA has only a thousand or so inspectors to examine millions of workplaces. OSHA inspections are more likely to occur after an accident or a complaint, but an internal inspection is possible without either of these things occurring. The best way to prepare your company for a visit from OSHA is to perform periodic internal safety inspections to test your compliance with health and safety regulations. An internal safety inspector could become safety manager to emphasize the importance of safe working conditions to the employees.

Other techniques can cut down on the adverse impact of an inspection. If you don't do so already, you should keep good records, particularly in terms of injuries to employees, and you should keep employees informed about the number of injuries that have occurred in the facility. Another strategy is to establish an active safety committee that is provided with good records about accidents and preventive activities established by the company. When an injury occurs, your records should list specific corrective steps that were taken to prevent the accident from happening again.

If an inspector shows up at your plant, you should strive not to create an adversarial relationship and you should treat the inspector professionally. One company fought to keep OSHA inspectors off its property for years. When the court finally ordered them allowed in, an adversarial relationship had already been established, and the inspection certainly was done by the book.

When the inspector arrives, you should provide your accident records to the inspector before they are requested, and you should ask the reason for the inspection (although the inspector may not reveal this information to you). During the inspection, assign your safety manager, or other well-trained employee, to accompany the inspector. Finally, ask for a conference with the inspector at the end of the inspection and attempt to determine the findings. Don't agree to anything that the inspector suggests that you find questionable. The internal inspections are important because they should help you prepare for the inspection and give you a rationale to provide to the inspector if any of your safety procedures or activities are challenged.

Additional References:

Atkinson, William (1999). When OSHA comes knocking. *HRMagazine*, October, Vol.44, No.10, p.34-38.

McNeese, Kathy & Balden-Anslyn, Roxanna (1998). Beyond OSHA 2000. *Occupational Health & Safety*, February, Vol.67, No.2, p.50-52.

JOB SAFETY & HEALTH PROTECTION

The Occupational Safety and Health Act of 1970 provides job safety and health protection for workers by promoting safe and healthful working conditions throughout the Nation. Provisions of the Act include the following:

Employers

All employers must furnish to employees employment and a place of employment free from recognized hazards that are causing or are likely to cause death or serious harm to employees. Employers must comply with occupational safety and health standards issued under the Act.

Employees

Employees must comply with all occupational safety and health standards, rules, regulations and orders issued under the Act that apply to their own actions and conduct on the job.

The Occupational Safety and Health Administration (OSHA) of the U.S. Department of Labor has the primary responsibility for administering the Act. OSHA issues occupational safety and health standards, and its Compliance Safety and Health Officers conduct jobsite inspections to help ensure compliance with the Act.

Inspection

The Act requires that a representative of the employer and a representative authorized by the employees be given an opportunity to accompany the OSHA inspector for the purpose of aiding the inspection.

Where there is no authorized employee representative, the OSHA Compliance Officer must consult with a reasonable number of employees concerning safety and health conditions in the workplace.

Complaint

Employees or their representatives have the right to file a complaint with the nearest OSHA office requesting an inspection if they believe unsafe or unhealthful conditions exist in their workplace. OSHA will withhold, on request, names of employees complaining.

The Act provides that employees may not be discharged or discriminated against in any way for filing safety and health complaints or for otherwise exercising their rights under the Act.

Employees who believe they have been discriminated against may file a complaint with their nearest OSHA office within 30 days of the alleged discriminatory action.

Citation

If upon inspection OSHA believes an employer has violated the Act, a citation alleging such violations will be issued to the employer. Each citation will specify a time period within which the alleged violation must be corrected.

The OSHA citation must be prominently displayed at or near the place of alleged violation for three days, or until it is corrected, whichever is later, to warn employees of dangers that may exist there.

Proposed Penalty

The Act provides for mandatory civil penalties against employers of up to $7,000 for each serious violation and for optional penalties of up to $7,000 for each nonserious violation. Penalties of up to $7,000 per day may be proposed for failure to correct violations within the proposed time period and for each day the violation continues beyond the prescribed abatement date. Also, any employer who willfully or repeatedly violates the Act may be assessed penalties of up to $70,000 for each such violation. A minimum penalty of $5,000 may be imposed for each willful violation. A violation of posting requirements can bring a penalty of up to $7,000.

There are also provisions for criminal penalties. Any willful violation resulting in the death of any employee, upon conviction, is punishable by a fine of up to $250,000 (or $500,000 if the employer is a corporation), or by imprisonment for up to six months, or both. A second conviction of an employer doubles the possible term of imprisonment. Falsifying records, reports, or applications is punishable by a fine of $10,000 or up to six months in jail or both.

Voluntary Activity

While providing penalties for violations, the Act also encourages efforts by labor and management, before an OSHA inspection, to reduce workplace hazards voluntarily and to develop and improve safety and health programs in all workplaces and industries. OSHA's Voluntary Protection Programs recognize outstanding efforts of this nature.

OSHA has published Safety and Health Program Management Guidelines to assist employers in establishing or perfecting programs to prevent or control employee exposure to workplace hazards. There are many public and private organizations that can provide information and assistance in this effort, if requested. Also, your local OSHA office can provide considerable help and advice on solving safety and health problems or can refer you to other sources for help such as training.

Consultation

Free assistance in identifying and correcting hazards and in improving safety and health management is available to employers, without citation or penalty, through OSHA-supported programs in each State. These programs are usually administered by the State Labor or Health department or a State university.

Posting Instructions

Employers in States operating OSHA approved State Plans should obtain and post the State's equivalent poster.

Under provisions of Title 29, Code of Federal Regulations, Part 1903.2(a)(1) employers must post this notice (or facsimile) in a conspicuous place where notices to employees are customarily posted.

More Information

Additional information and copies of the Act, specific OSHA safety and health standards, and other applicable regulations may be obtained from your employer or from the nearest OSHA Regional Office in the following locations:

Atlanta, GA	(404) 347-3573
Boston, MA	(617) 565-7164
Chicago, IL	(312) 353-2220
Dallas, TX	(214) 767-4731
Denver, CO	(303) 391-5858
Kansas City, MO	(816) 426-5861
New York, NY	(212) 337-2378
Philadelphia, PA	(215) 596-1201
San Francisco, CA	(415) 744-6670
Seattle, WA	(206) 553-5930

Robert B. Reich, Secretary of Labor

U.S. Department of Labor

Occupational Safety and Health Administration

Washington, DC 1995 (Reprinted) OSHA 2203

This information will be made available to sensory impaired individuals upon request. Voice phone: (202) 219-9615; TDD message referral phone: 1-800-326-2577

GPO: 1995 0 - 163-097 QL 3

Washington, DC
1995 (Reprinted)
OSHA 2203

130

Overtime

In an all-salaried workforce, both exempt employees, who traditionally are paid a salary rather than an hourly rate, and nonexempt employees receive a prescribed amount of money each pay period that does not primarily depend on the number of hours worked.

Although there has been a dramatic increase in the number of companies that have recently moved to an all-salaried compensation plan, this strategy won't help your overtime situation. In fact, it usually increases your payroll expenses because you are guaranteeing a fixed-base salary regardless if the employee works 35 hours during a given week or 40 hours. Most important to understand is that even when this nonexempt employee is placed on a salary, you are still required to pay overtime (1.5 times normal pay) for every hour worked over 40.

So why has there been an increase in companies going this compensation route? Companies who operate all-salaried workforces usually do so with the intent of eliminating the "us" versus "them" attitude that sometimes separates the exempt from the nonexempt employees. Some organizations believe that the two-class distinction will never encourage lower-level employees to feel empowered, share management aspirations, or be truly committed to the organization. So the advantages of an all-salaried workforce are not in cost savings but rather in increased loyalty and commitment to the organization.

To reduce your overtime expenses, it might be more fruitful to investigate the use of temporary employees to supplement your existing workforce during peak demand periods. The calculation of overtime for nonexempts is not always as easy as it may seem. So we suggest you consult the interpretative bulletins provided free of charge by the Wage and Hour Division of the U.S. Department of Labor before you make any specific changes.

Additional References:

Dean, Rebecca & Smith, Matthew (1996). Fix it now—before your employees fix it for you: How to conduct a wage and hour self-audit. *Employee Relations Law Journal*, Autumn, Vol.22, No.2, p. 31-55.

Hartinger, Arthur A. (1997). Fair Labor Standards Act: 1996 salary basis test update. *Government Finance Review*, February, Vol.13, No.1, p.29-31.

Martin, Christopher L., Aalberts, Robert J., & Clark, Lawrence S. (1993). The FLSA and the fluctuating workweek scheme: Competitive strategy or worker exploitation. *Labor Law Journal*, Vol. 44, No. 2, p. 22-38.

Your Rights Under the Fair Labor Standards Act

Federal Minimum Wage

$4.75 per hour
beginning October 1, 1996

$5.15 per hour
beginning September 1, 1997

Employees under 20 years of age may be paid $4.25 per hour during their first 90 consecutive calendar days of employment with an employer.

Certain full-time students, student learners, apprentices, and workers with disabilities may be paid less than the minimum wage under special certificates issued by the Department of Labor.

<u>Tip Credit</u> – Employers of "tipped employees" must pay a cash wage of at least $2.13 per hour if they claim a tip credit against their minimum wage obligation. If an employee's tips combined with the employer's cash wage of at least $2.13 per hour do not equal the minimum hourly wage, the employer must make up the difference. Certain other conditions must also be met.

Overtime Pay

At least $1^1/_2$ times your regular rate of pay for all hours worked over 40 in a workweek.

Child Labor

An employee must be at least **16** years old to work in most non-farm jobs and at least **18** to work in non-farm jobs declared hazardous by the Secretary of Labor. Youths **14** and **15** years old may work outside school hours in various non-manufacturing, non-mining, non-hazardous jobs under the following conditions:

No more than –
- **3** hours on a school day or **18** hours in a school week;
- **8** hours on a non-school day or **40** hours in a non-school week.

Also, work may not begin before **7 a.m.** or end after **7 p.m.**, except from **June 1** through **Labor Day**, when evening hours are extended to **9 p.m.** Different rules apply in agricultural employment.

Enforcement

The Department of Labor may recover back wages either administratively or through court action, for the employees that have been underpaid in violation of the law. Violations may result in civil or criminal action.

Fines of up to $10,000 per violation may be assessed against employers who violate the child labor provisions of the law and up to $1,000 per violation against employers who willfully or repeatedly violate the minimum wage or overtime pay provisions. This law <u>prohibits</u> discriminating against or discharging workers who file a complaint or participate in any proceedings under the Act.

Note: • Certain occupations and establishments are exempt from the minimum wage and/or overtime pay provisions.
• Special provisions apply to workers in American Samoa.
• Where state law requires a higher minimum wage, the higher standard applies.

For Additional Information, Contact the Wage and Hour Division office nearest you — listed in your telephone directory under United States Government, Labor Department.

This poster may be viewed on the world wide web at this address: http://www.dol.gov/dol/esa/public/minwage/main.htm

The law requires employers to display this poster where employees can readily see it.

U.S. Department of Labor
Employment Standards Administration
Wage and Hour Division
Washington, D.C. 20210

WH Publication 1088
Revised October 1996

P

Pay secrecy

 Although most employees are not told what their co-workers are being paid, over the past several years, most organizations have increased the amount of information they have provided employees in regard to their pay. Most frequently communicated information included the following: the quality and advantages of overall pay policies; pay ranges for the individual's current position and for all jobs in a typical career path to which employees could logically aspire; how these ranges were established; and typical pay increases that could be expected for poor, satisfactory, and top performance.

Several reasons are typically given for communicating pay information of this type. First, for managers and employees to gain an accurate view of the pay system and for the compensation system to motivate effective performance, they need to be informed. In addition, there is evidence that the goodwill engendered by the act of being open about pay not only increases the perception that the pay is fair, but that the organization in general acts fairly. For example, in organizations with secret pay plans, we often hear comments such as "If the pay system really is fair, what have you got to hide? . . . If you're hiding something about pay, can we trust you at all?" Perhaps the most important information to be communicated is the work-related and business-related rationale on which the system is based. Some employees may not agree with these rationales or the results, but at least they will be clear that pay is determined on something other than the whims and biases of their supervisors.

Whether an open, heavily communicated pay plan is more effective than a closed pay plan where secrecy prevails depends largely on how much effort has been devoted by your company to design a fair and equitable compensation system, with this sound rationale. Such a strategy should enhance employees' motivation and help to retain top performers, which are prime objectives of pay systems. However, if the pay system is not based on work-related or business-related logic, then the wisest course of action may be to minimize the formal and informal discussion of pay and pay policy . . . until the secret pay system can be put in order.

Additional References:

Anonymous (1992). Handbook rule against wage discussion illegal. *Mountain States Employers Council Bulletin*, February, p.1.

Bartol, K. M. & Martin, D. C. (1989). Effects of dependency, dependency threats, and pay secrecy. *Journal of Applied Psychology*, Vol.74, No.1, p.105-113.

McFarlin, Dean B, & Fron, Michael R. (1990). A two-tier wage structure in a nonunion firm. *Industrial Relations*, Winter, Vol..29, No.1, p.145-154.

Performance evaluation & the angry

employee

 As you noted from speaking with your colleagues, defensive behavior is a fairly normal reaction to being confronted with a criticism. Defensive behaviors can include denial of a problem area, anger, or even retreating into a shell. Although normal, these coping behaviors undermine the usefulness of the performance appraisal process and they postpone the employee's ability to effectively deal with the problem. Two situations that seem to increase the likelihood of these defensive coping strategies are instances where the employee's dignity and self-worth are challenged and those situations where the criticism catches the employee totally by surprise.

Part of the reason employees may feel caught "off guard" can be explained by the amount of emphasis many managers place on the annual feedback sessions as opposed to providing continual feedback over the course of a year. If you're giving daily, weekly, or monthly feedback, there will be no surprises at the once-a-year formal review. Other managers seem skilled at providing the continual feedback, but only when the feedback is positive. Positive reinforcement is one of the most powerful tools used to shape behavior in the desired direction. However, the reluctance on a manager's part to provide similar year-round feedback focused on individual weaknesses or problem areas can lead employees to believe that their problems are relatively unimportant. Either type of manager will create the element of surprise at the annual review, which can foster defensiveness.

You'll also need to closely examine what took place during those annual performance review sessions. This is where you have a direct effect on the employee's sense of dignity and self-worth. For example, you should give performance feedback in private and allow enough time for the employee to discuss issues important to him or her. Failure to listen to the employee and encourage participation can lead to a feeling of unfairness. Without "voice," employees often perceive that they have not had the opportunity to discuss important constraints outside their control that may have lowered their performance. Could this focus on employee "voice" lead to a whining session? Perhaps, but providing "voice" will be extremely effective as a strategy to reduce the defensiveness with which you are concerned. As a side benefit, it also may heighten two-way communication leading both you and your employee to focus on performance weaknesses as a common problem to be solved in a joint effort.

Additional References:

Dunnette, Marvin D. (1993). My hammer or your hammer? *Human Resource Management*, Summer-Fall, Vol.32, No.2-3, p.373-384.

Thomas, Steven L. and Bretz, Robert D., Jr. (1994). Research and practice in performance appraisal: Evaluating employee performance in America's largest companies. *SAM Advanced Management Journal*, Spring, Vol.59, No.2, p.28-34.

Performance feedback & career

development

Your boss's desire to help his employees grow is both a noble and a wise business decision. It sounds like a good place to start is with the aforementioned supervisor, as well as other supervisors at your company. We suggest that a management development program is a crucial first step in implementing the new program your boss desires.

This program would involve training the problem manager and other managers in effective supervisory and interpersonal skills. Is it possible that this supervisor has no tact because no one has taken the time to work with her and show her the importance of dealing with those she supervises in a considerate manner? Is it possible that her supervisor treats her with no tact and she is emulating her boss? Relatively inexpensive outside seminars and workshops in supervision are readily available to bring management people along. If there is only one problem supervisor, you may consider individual instruction for that employee.

Once you have provided the supervisors with some training, it is up to the CEO and other top managers to model acceptable management techniques by practicing them in front of all employees. That is, management should lead by example. The CEO must make clear the expectation that these techniques are expected of all supervisors.

We also recommend that a system of rewards and demerits be developed as part of the reinforcement process. Rewards are a very effective means of shaping and changing behavior. With this thought in mind, we further suggest that your boss tie the new development program a little closer to the system of determining pay raises.

If the problem supervisor does not adapt to these changes within a reasonable period of time, then you must consider whether that person should remain as a supervisor. The value of the performance appraisal process is often undermined by exactly the problem you have presented here. Let the CEO know that the extra time and resources spent training your managers will pay dividends in developing the rest of the staff.

Additional References:

Coates, Dennis E. (1998). Don't tie 360 feedback to pay. *Training*, September, Vol.35, No.9, p.68-74.

Scandura, T. (1992). Mentorship and career mobility: an empirical investigation. *Journal of Organizational Behavior,* Vol.13, No..2, p.169-172.

Thomas, Steven L. (1997). Performance appraisals: Any use for training? *Business Forum*, Winter, Vol.22, No.1, p. 9-32.

Personality conflicts

 Mary Ellen sounds like she's quite high in a personality dimension called Machiavellianism. The concept is named after Niccolo Machiavelli, the 16th century author of *The Prince*, a book on how noblemen should acquire and use power. Among the guiding principles Machiavelli recommended were the following:

- Never show humility—arrogance is far more effective when dealing with others.
- Morality and ethics are for the weak.
- It is much better to be feared than loved.

Questionnaires exist to measure each person's orientation toward Machiavellianism. Surprisingly, research has found that people with a Machiavellian orientation are quite common.

People who are high in this personality dimension are pragmatic, are capable of lying and manipulation to achieve personal goals, are more likely to take control in loosely structured situations, and are more apt to win in win–lose situations. They often possess characteristics associated with confidence, eloquence, and competence.

These traits combined with their pure pragmatism can be devastating. Although personality has a basis in biology, it develops in people as a product of their social and cultural environments. It is probable that Mary Ellen's family background, social class, educational background, and previous work background contribute to her Machiavellian tendencies just as these factors would contribute to other dimensions of her personality, such as her creativity.

Personality is an important factor to consider in work situations; behavior of employees cannot be understood without considering personality.

When Mary Ellen was promoted, her managers may or may not have viewed her personality as important. Obviously, it will be a factor in her success as a supervisor; she will find it very difficult to achieve work group goals if all of her employees hate her manipulative nature. Yet, on the bright side, the pragmatism of the person high in Machiavellianism may lead Mary Ellen to change her conniving ways so as to encourage you to help her achieve your group's goals.

What can you do if you encounter Machiavellian behavior in the future? One effective means involves exposing this unprincipled behavior to others. Once the actions of Machiavellian types are made public within an organization, it is much harder to use manipulative tactics or dirty tricks in the future. These individuals also have the edge when emotions run high, or when others are uncertain how to proceed. The Machiavellian individual realizes that under such conditions, many people will be distracted and less likely to realize that they are being manipulated for someone else's gain. If you can't avoid such a situation, at least don't make important decisions or commitments at that time.

Additional References:

Behling, Orlando (1998). Employee selection: Will intelligence and conscientiousness do the job? *The Academy of Management Executive*, February, Vol.12, No.1, p. 77-86.

Mudrack, Peter E. (1993). An investigation into the acceptability of workplace behaviors of a dubious ethical nature. *Journal of Business Ethics*, Vol.12, p.517-524.

Pregnant employees

 A little flexibility is in order to help you work through this problem, which is a management question and not a legal one at this point. It seems that you are facing the loss of half of your staff, at least for a few months next year, and you want to let two good employees go and hire two rookies rather than consider a very simple alternative.

That alternative is job sharing. If you allow each of your new moms to work a few hours each day or two or three days a week (splitting the hours and days between them), you can allow them to share one position and hire only one new person. This approach permits you to retain both of these good employees and keep training and learning costs lower by assimilating only one new hire into the operation.

Many companies of larger size than yours make frequent use of job sharing. Research indicates that job-sharing programs tend to reduce turnover and absenteeism, to increase morale, and in larger companies to help reach the organization's affirmative action goals. A key element to the program's success is your ability to coordinate the work of the two job sharers. In a tight labor market such as the one we have been experiencing, it is crucial to retain the best employees, and this may be done through flexible, creative thinking. You can contact a temp agency to bring potential new hires on board before these women begin their maternity leaves and the women can assist in the training. A temp also may help bridge the gap between the women's maternity leaves and when they return to work part time. In many cases, the working mother might seek a return to full-time status in a few years. If you have made accommodations to help good employees through this sort of flexibility, you are building long-term loyalty toward your organization. You also have kept your costs under control and staffed your office as needed.

Additional References:

Burns, James (1997). Accommodating pregnant employees. *Employee Relations Law Journal*, Vol.23, No.1, p.139-144.

Sheley, Elizabeth (1996). Job sharing offers unique challenges. *HRMagazine*, January, Vol.41, No.1, p.46-49.

Privacy & HRIS

 Balancing the employer's legitimate right to make certain information available to those in the organization who need it, with the employee's right to privacy, is often not as easy as it would seem. Legislation such as the Federal Privacy Act gives some employees legal rights regarding who has access to information about their work history and job performance. However, the act does not specifically address access to phone numbers or addresses of employees.

Because of a concern over privacy, many organizations grant information access on a need-to-know basis. Access matrices are incorporated into the software of most data base management systems and define the rights of various users to each element contained in the database. We can think of many legitimate reasons why your unpublished phone number may be required by many individuals in a company. Further, it is not unusual for such a listing you describe to be published. However, most companies that make addresses and phone numbers available ask the employees first, as a courtesy, and do not publish the phone number if it is so desired. That's not to imply that those who really need to phone you at home can't do so. Your number is simply not available to anyone who might want to reach you for nonbusiness reasons.

Additional References:

Bland-Acosta, Barbara A. (1988). Developing an HRIS privacy policy. *Personnel Administrator*, July, Vol.33, No.7, p52-57.

O'Connell, Sandra E. (1994). Security for HR records. *HR Magazine*, September, Vol.39, No.9, p.37-40.

Promotion from within

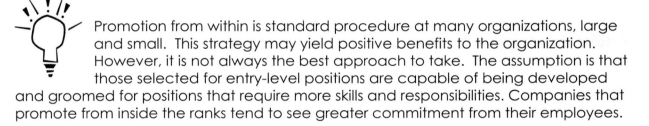

Promotion from within is standard procedure at many organizations, large and small. This strategy may yield positive benefits to the organization. However, it is not always the best approach to take. The assumption is that those selected for entry-level positions are capable of being developed and groomed for positions that require more skills and responsibilities. Companies that promote from inside the ranks tend to see greater commitment from their employees.

Unfortunately, as more companies move to self-directed teams, there are fewer opportunities for promotion to a supervisory position because there are fewer management positions available. This is occurring at the same time that large numbers of employees are reaching the point in their careers when they believe it is their turn to be promoted.   Companies that want to build and retain commitment to these employees must figure out alternative ways to provide them growth opportunities in their jobs.

Further, it should not be assumed that because an employee is loyal to his employer or highly committed to the organization, he or she has the skills and abilities to succeed in a higher-level position.

If an organization expects positive benefits from a promotion-from-within strategy, three critical steps must be taken. First, organizations must make sure they hire people who have promotion potential. Then education and training must be provided to help employees realize their potential to be promoted. Finally, career-oriented performance appraisals are required. You and your employer must link your past performance, your career performance, and developmental needs in a formal career plan.

Keep in mind that recruiting and promoting from inside the company does have its negatives as well. Employees who apply for promotions and don't receive them may become disgruntled, particularly if they view the process as a charade because the manager has already decided who they want to hire for the job (e.g., "The Good Old Boy Network"). In addition, promoting internal candidates can lead to inbreeding; a lack of new ideas and alternative approaches to solving problems can occur if all of the supervisors have been brought up through the ranks. We've witnessed many lost opportunities and organizational failures associated with organizational inbreeding and maintaining the status quo.

As a manager who has been passed over for promotion, you may want to sit down with your boss to discuss your career goals and see if you can realize them by staying with this particular company. Be sure to inquire as to whether the company will support you (perhaps through a tuition reimbursement program) to get the training and skills you need to rise through the ranks. If your goals are incompatible with this company's objectives, you may want to consider your options. There are many organizations that need good managers.

Additional References:

Chan, William (1996). External recruitment versus internal promotion. *Journal of Labor Economics*, Vol.14, p.555-570.

Laabs, Jennifer J. (1993). Business growth driven by staff development. *Personnel Journal*, April, Vol.72, No.4, p.120-129.

Promotion to management

 This is a tricky problem and one that could ruin not only your personal relationships with your co-workers but also your effectiveness as a manager—if you don't handle it properly.

A great deal depends on previous relationships with your co-workers, whether you got along well with them, whether one or more feel slighted because they did not get the job, whether they are pleased with the owner's choice of you as office manager. It is important not to make the transition to supervisor too abruptly and create hostility in the office by making your co-workers feel slighted. However, it is important for you to establish that you are now in charge of the office and they should not take advantage of you. This can be done in subtle ways, rather than via directives and memos.

You want to influence your co-workers toward the accomplishment of the organization's goals; this does not mean barking orders and trying to find fault in everything they do. Only a small part of the influence you possess flows from the authority of your new position. There are other power sources that can help you influence those you are supervising. You gain influence from your ability to reward or punish employees, from your expertise at what you do, and from your personal appeal as a likable person. Analyze yourself and see which of these sources can be strengths. For example, does the owner give you responsibility to make decisions regarding extra rewards for a job well done? Or are you a legitimate expert about the work in the office? Or do your co-workers generally like and respect you?

It is crucial at the start to meet with each worker individually and discuss the strengths that person possesses and how those capabilities will help in the office. At this point, it is important to question the workers, attempt to find out their concerns, and figure out how you may be able to respond to these concerns. From these initial conversations, you may get some insight into how the staff perceives your promotion, whether your co-workers will respect you in your new job, and what sources of power might help you gain the level of influence you need for success.

It is important for you to figure out why you have been given this job and what level of support you can expect from the owner of the business. Will the owner back you in making a tough decision regarding one of your workers? Will the owner allow you to reward the workers for a job well done, or will you only be allowed to punish failure? The backing of your boss is important, and you must determine how much support you have as you go into the job. To succeed, you will need support from above and below, and you will need to project competence as well as concern for your employees.

Additional References:

Masciarelli, James P. (1998). Managing staff relationships. *HR Focus*, August, Vol.75, No.8, p.1.

Wayne, Sandy J., Liden, Robert C., Graf, Isabel K. & Ferris, Gerald R. (1997). The role of upward influence tactics in human resource decisions. *Personnel Psychology*, Vol.50, p.979-1006.

Q

Quality management during a downsizing

 Your concerns are not unfounded. The incompatibility of a continuous quality improvement program and organizational downsizing seems obvious. TQM takes a long-term perspective, requiring a series of incremental improvements. With TQM, or any other continuous improvement program, management's role is to demonstrate the commitment essential to motivate employees to actively participate. Gaining the commitment of the employees and encouraging initiative, improvement, and innovation likely require that employees feel secure in their jobs. In contrast, downsizing is a radical action that is usually carried out quickly and decisively by top management and creates high levels of insecurity.

However, a series of studies have found that if the downsizing is handled properly, TQM-type programs will continue to flourish. By "properly handled" we mean that the layoff notification should be delivered with adequate, open, and truthful communication. In fact, layoffs were less devastating in organizations with TQM programs, because good communication and trust between management and the workforce was in place before the bad news of layoffs occurred.

So, if your TQM program is being implemented properly, the effect of your proposed layoff may be less severe than if no quality programs existed; just keep those lines of communication open.

Additional References:

Brockner, J., Siegel, P., Daly, J., Tyler, T., & Martin, C. (1997). When trust matters: The moderating effect of outcome favorability. *Administrative Science Quarterly*, Vol. 42, No. 3, p.558-583.

Dean, J. & Evans, J. (1994). *Total Quality Management, Organization, & Strategy*. Minneapolis: West Publishing Company.

R

Reference checks

 Many companies have a strict policy to provide as little information as possible to those checking references of current and past employees because they fear a lawsuit either from the individual or from the company conducting the reference check. Without written consent of the individual, some companies will confirm only employment and/or the dates of employment. Guidelines also suggest that those contacted for references not volunteer information and avoid vague statements about the individual.

Those providing responses to reference checks often face being put between the proverbial "rock and a hard place." For example, suppose you had once documented an automobile accident involving one of your employees and the company car. You had good reason to believe alcohol was involved. The individual subsequently left your organization and his potential new employer asked you for a reference. If you reported the drinking incident during the reference check process, you may have faced a defamation of character suit from the former employee. If, when asked, you did not divulge the incident to the employer and that employee was again involved in a similar accident under his new employer, you may have been sued by the new employer for negligence.

Managers faced with the inability to provide relevant information to prospective new employers received some relief when numerous state legislatures passed bills pertaining to the disclosure of employment information. The legislation, sought by state and national human resource management lobbies, enabled employers to provide to other prospective employers accurate information about a current or former employee's job performance or the employee's reason for leaving the organization. They may do so without fear of liability—either for defamation or for negligence—if the employer is not acting in bad faith. Bad faith means there is significant evidence that the employer disclosed information knowing it was "false and deliberately misleading." As defined by the new law, "job performance" includes such factors as attendance, attitude, awards, demotions, duties, effort, evaluations, knowledge, skills, promotions, and disciplinary actions.

Although the new law provides wide latitude for employers in many states to provide a truthful reference about a current or former employee, the key is making an effort to be truthful and to act in good faith. For example, if a negative performance appraisal was given to an employee and the employee wrote a rebuttal disputing the appraisal, the good faith provision might suggest disclosing that the employee disputed the negative appraisal. Regardless, it is important to have a policy and guidelines in place for disclosure of information and to make sure that accurate information is released only to those who have a specific need to receive the information, that is, prospective employers.

Additional References:

Siegel, Robert A. & Garrett, Anne E. (1998). Giving employee references: potential pitfalls and protections. *Los Angeles Business Journal*, January 12, Vol.20, No.2, p.25.

Sommars, Jack (1998). The truth is out there: How to check job applicants' backgrounds. *Colorado Business Magazine*, June, Vol.25, No.6, p.70-71.

Religion & Muzak® in the office

Because your boss is a private—not a public—employer, he may play religious music in the office and hold moments of silence, even if it makes employees sick. He apparently has established a strong set of values that he would like employees to share. However, you may not share those values, and there is a lack of fit between you and the organization. This mismatch may have a negative impact on your performance to the detriment of you and your employer, something he might want to consider before broadcasting the next sermon.

Title VII of the Civil Rights Act protects employees from being discriminated against in hiring, promotion, or tenure on the basis of religion. If you decided to complain about the music because it violates your religious beliefs and were later denied promotion or were fired, you may have a case that your civil rights were violated.

Additional References:

Cromwell, Jeff B. (1997). Cultural discrimination: The reasonable accommodation of religion in the workplace. *Employee Responsibilities and Rights Journal*, Vol.10, p.155-173.

Malone, Michael D., Hartman, Sandra J. & Payne, Dinah (1998). Religion in the workplace: How much is too much? *Labor Law Journal*, June, Vol.49, No.6, p.1074-1081.

Religious holidays & accommodation

The EEOC does have guidelines addressing the necessity to accommodate employee observation of religious holidays. Employers are required to consider alternative ways to accommodate religious practices, such as holiday observances, unless such accommodation would cause undue business hardship. Possible means of accommodation include soliciting voluntary substitutes from another shift, swapping employee hours, changing employees' job assignments, using flexible work breaks, exchanging lunchtime for early departure, or making temporary overtime payments to fill the void. In accommodating an employee's religious practices, employers are not required to choose the option the employee prefers, as long as the employer's offer is reasonable. Further, employers should not be expected to incur regular and repeated overtime costs to replace an employee who will not work on a Sabbath, or when a large number of employees must take off on the same day.

Given that you had two employees stating that it was against their religious beliefs to work on Christmas, we believe you did the right thing when you backed down and sought alternative employees to fill in. If 100 people asked for the day off, we would view the situation as a hardship, because you'd probably have to shut down the business. Still, there is the expectation that you try to accommodate even in that extreme of a situation. For example if you can be down only 10 employees and 100 want off, those 10 employees with the most seniority could be given first pick of the schedule. Alternatively, you could establish a lottery to determine the 10. In either case, you can't be accused of not accommodating at all.

Additional References:

http://www.eeoc.gov/facts/fs-relig.html

Zachary, Mary-Kathryn (1996). Handling religious expression in the workplace. *Supervision*, December, Vol.57, No.12, p.5-7.

Repatriation

Some organizations report a 30 to 40 percent turnover by managers after they complete an international assignment. In some companies, the turnover rate can reach 70 percent. Of course, some of these managers leave because, after they complete an overseas assignment, they become more marketable and develop more contacts. In other cases, the managers leave because of difficulties that are typical of a repatriated manager. These problems include loss of a financial premium paid on their overseas assignments, the fact that the United States is now a foreign culture to them because they are acclimated to the culture of the country where they had been assigned, and the feeling that their assignments upon return do not have the status of their foreign assignments.

Whatever the turnover rate and its causes, there is a strong potential to lose Constance and other repatriated managers soon after they return unless the company pays a great deal of attention to integrating them back into the flow of the organization. Losses such as these are very costly, particularly after the company has invested as much as three times an individual's salary to send them on an overseas assignment in the first place.

To successfully reintegrate the repatriated manager, the company must consider how it will handle the expatriate manager's return *before* that person is sent overseas. Firms and potential expatriate managers should discuss the manager's career goals and how the assignment will fit into the goals as part of the selection process. If this understanding can be reached before the assignment is made, the reentry into domestic operations might go more smoothly. Several global companies also appoint a home-office sponsor to help manage the expatriate manager's career interests while that employee is on the assignment. Finally, many companies are sensitive to the financial loss of the overseas premium so they provide some financial assistance to ease the repatriated manager's transition back into the home country. Your question indicates that this overseas assignment has had a positive effect on Constance's career, so it appears your company has planned and managed her career effectively.

The problem your company has is different: how to handle the employees who have remained in the home office while Constance was enhancing her career overseas. One suggestion is to make it clear to those employees that one way to boost their own careers is to pursue an expatriate assignment. Constance is a good example for them. Her overseas assignment led her to receive a promotion and those who are grousing about it could put themselves in line for career growth by gaining similar experience. If international experience is the implicit way to advance in the organization, this element of company strategy should be made explicit.

Another suggestion for improving the home office morale is to explain the successes achieved by Constance as head of the European operation and to make clear the contributions that the division makes to the bottom line. Many large corporations gain more than half of their revenues from overseas operations. If the international contribution to your company's success is clarified, it should dispel the notion that Constance is returning from an extended vacation.

Additional References:

Carey, Patricia M. (1998). Expatriate games. *Working Woman,* May, Vol.23, No.5, p.106-107.

Feldman D.C. & Thompson, J.T. (1993). Expatriation, repatriation, and domestic geographical relocation: An empirical investigation of adjustment to new job assignments. *Journal of International Business Studies,* Vol.24, p.507-529.

Solomon, Charlene M. (1995). Repatriation: Up, down or out? *Personnel Journal,* January, Vol.74, No.1, p. 28.

Romance in the workplace

 Before you take action, you need to consider why you believe the marriage will cause problems and if it will indeed cause difficulties. There were apparently no problems while these two managers were dating. Why would marriage change the situation? If these two are talented managers, it appears that your most damaging course of action would be to ask one of them to leave. The manager who leaves may go to work for a competitor in the same business, and this can create an even more ticklish situation.

According to a recent SHRM survey, less that 30 percent of organizations have established policies that forbid employees from dating or that prohibit married couples from working in the same company. The majority of companies surveyed choose to avoid the issue of romance in the workplace altogether.

Yet, it may be unwise to skirt the issue because the changing demographics of the workforce—more women, more single mothers—dictate that these sorts of occurrences are likely to increase. According to John Challenger, CEO of the job outplacement firm Challenger, Gray & Christmas, "More and more, the workplace in the new millenium has become what singles bars were in the 1970s, what health clubs were in the 1980s and what Internet liaisons were in the 1990s for taking a romantic chance." Of course, not all romances are going to progress to marriage.

Off limits are relationships between a subordinate and a supervisor, which, while not the issue you present, have a high potential for appearance of impropriety to co-workers and others and could lead to charges of sexual harassment.

While there are dilemmas stemming from office romances, such as increased potential for conflict, there can be positive results as well: more teamwork, improved communications, and increased productivity. Although research appears to indicate that most romantic relationships have little impact on the work habits of the participants, perceptions of co-workers are often affected. Managing these perceptions in a positive direction by the two managers and by you, as their boss, may be your greatest challenge.

Additional References:

Mainiero, Lisa A. (1986). A review and analysis of power dynamics in organizational romances. *Academy of Management Review*, October, Vol.11, No.4, p.750-762.

Paul, Robert J. & Townsend, James B. (1998). Managing the workplace romance: Protecting employee and employer rights. *Review of Business*, Winter, Vol.19, No.2, p.25-30.

S

"Salting"

 Yes, salting is legal despite its appearance. What can happen is this: A union member will apply to your company for a job and make it clear that he is a union member, almost daring you not to hire him. If you don't hire him, he can claim that you are discriminating against him because he is a union member and file a complaint with the National Labor Relations Board. And if you hire him, he will try to get fired. Again, the result is a complaint against you for firing him *because* he is a union member.

A variant of this tactic that is used for union organizing is for the applicant to keep union membership secret and attempt to get hired by the company. Once inside the company, the union member starts an organizing drive. If you fire him for doing that, you are afoul of federal labor law. Unions who want to organize a company sometimes salt a few workers into the company secretly to assist in their efforts. Actions taken against these workers result in complaints to the NLRB. Again, this use of salting is legal.

According to *Investor's Business Daily* (June 24, 1998), one of the victims of union salting activities was Manno Electric, Inc., of Baton Rouge, Louisiana. The newspaper gave this account of what happened to this $1-million-a-year company, which employs about a dozen electricians:

About six years ago, the owner's son-in-law, who was an officer of the company, was approached by several members of a union local who sought jobs with the firm. The company had no job openings at the time. The applicants asked the son-in-law why he did not like unions. The company official provided his opinions about unions and why the company did not have them. These comments were secretly tape recorded by the union members.

The union filed a complaint about the comments, and the NLRB found the remarks to be discrimination against the union, which is an unfair labor practice. The findings resulted in fines for damages and back pay of nearly $800,000 against the company plus its own legal fees. The company's appeals were turned down in the courts, and the company struggled to pay the fines and legal fees.

Our advice to you is to keep any discussion of union membership or feelings about unions to yourself and not discuss them with applicants or workers. There are too many risks of being accused of discrimination and unfair labor practices to be candid in your feelings about unions. Just continue to treat your people well. There is no need to explain why you are doing so.

One potential defense in salting cases is to ask each applicant to fill out an application form that requests previous employment activities and other information from the employee. You should state on the form that answering questions falsely is grounds for dismissal and have the applicant sign it. If you discover that the person you hired is a union salt, examine the application form for false statements. Dismissing an employee for making false statements on a legitimate application form would be a defense against charges of anti-union discrimination.

Legislation to deal with the potential abuse of labor laws by unions is pending in Congress. The Truth in Employment Act would state that employers aren't required to hire workers seeking jobs under false pretenses. The bill also would shift the burden of proof to the NLRB to show that the employer discriminated against the union member. Finally, small firms such as yours would be reimbursed for attorneys' fees if they win such a case.

Additional References:

Fine, Cory R. (1998). Beware the Trojan horse. *Workforce*. Vol.77,No.5, p.44-50.

Hess, Gary E. (1997). Salting: An industry perspective. *Journal of Labor Research*, Vol.18, p.47-54.

Sexual harassment

Even though the party took place in your home, if it is an officially sanctioned office party, the event you describe could reflect a hostile work environment and lead to a claim of sexual harassment. All complaints about sexual harassment must be taken seriously. As one sexual harassment manual for supervisors and managers advises, "When confronted with sexual harassment complaints or when inappropriate sexual conduct is observed in the workplace, the best reaction is to address the complaint and stop the conduct immediately." Remember, an employee's co-workers or even the employer's customers can cause the employer to be held responsible for sexual harassment and the harassment does not have to have tangible consequences such as demotion or termination.

Additional References:

Flynn, G. (1997). A pioneer program nurtures a harassment free workplace. *Workforce,* October, p.38-43.

Grimsley, Kirstin Downey (1998). For employers, a blunt warning. *The Washington Post,* June 27, Vol.121, p.A10, col.1.

Segal, Jonathan A. (1997). The catch-22s of remedying sexual harassment complaints. *HRMagazine,* October, Vol.42, No.10, p.111-117.

Sick leave banks

The donations your friend spoke of are becoming more common in organizations. Sick leave banks are a good way to let employees help each other out by donating their vacation time to fellow employees who have exhausted all sick and vacation time due to a catastrophic illness. Most programs work along the following lines: The employee must first submit a request to a sick leave bank board of directors, who decide whether to grant the request and how many days of sick leave will be granted. In some organizations the manager from the recipient's area quietly spreads the word and asks for donations. In other companies, the employees donate one to three days by checking a payroll deduction box at the beginning of the year. Some companies convert the days to dollars and then back to days so as to reflect the actual cost of the sick day. Other companies prefer not to get into this kind of bookkeeping, so individuals receive one day for every day donated. As with any program of this kind, things can get complicated quickly and before setting up a program you need to do your research. But we believe it is worth the effort.

Additional Reference:

Zweiback, Richard (1995). Curbing sick leave losses. *School and College*, February, Vol.34, No.2, p.32-33.

"Slackers" & withholding effort on a team

 One of the potential disadvantages of working in teams is that some of the group members might gain benefits without doing any work. Your previous experience with Bill indicates that he's engaging in free riding on tasks in which he does not gain a personal reward. Apparently, Bill could hide in the crowd when being supervised by a manager and get away with lack of effort. His fellow wait staff did not turn him in; now under the new system you are responsible for seeing that he does his share of the work.

The key ingredients are team norms, the standards of conduct that are expected of each member of the group. The goal for you and your co-workers is establishing group norms of high performance and shared duties at the outset of the new supervisory set-up. Research indicates that the first behaviors that occur in a group set a precedent for what is expected later. To establish norms of shared responsibility and high effort, you and your teammates must establish that everyone does a full share of the work and slackers will not be tolerated. For example, all team members are expected to bus tables, fill water glasses, and participate in general clean-up at closing time.

The "new order" will conflict with Bill's attempt to carry over behaviors that worked for him under the previous supervisor. To enforce the new norms, you and your teammates may want to split tips based on the performance of each team member. Once Bill is shorted a few times, his behavior may change. It is important that all members of the team pressure Bill to get with the program.

Additional References:

Duff, Christina (1998). It's sad but true: Good times are bad for real slackers. *Wall Street Journal*, August 6, Vol.232, No.26, p.A1,

Kidwell Jr., Roland E. & Bennett, Nathan (1993). Employee propensity to withhold effort: A conceptual model to intersect three avenues of research. *Academy of Management Review*, Vol.18, p.429-456.

Mulvey, Paul W. & Klein, Howard J. (1998). Impact of perceived loafing and collective efficacy on group goal processes and group performance. *Organizational Behavior & Human Decision Processes*, Vol.74, p.62-87.

Smokers

 Numerous studies have attempted to quantify the dollar costs associated with employing smokers. Factors contributing to these higher costs have included increased health coverage, a higher morbidity rate, increased absenteeism rates, and even increased accident rates. Although it is not clear why accidents on the job would be higher for smokers compared with nonsmokers, researchers have hypothesized that if smokers are willing to risk their health with the use of tobacco, they may be willing to take other risks involving workplace safety.

Although the methodology, statistics, and conclusions drawn from most of the studies linking smoking with increased organizational costs have been questioned, some employers give preference to applicants who do not smoke, or actually have a policy that requires that only nonsmokers be hired.

The Americans with Disabilities Act prohibits employers from discriminating against rehabilitated alcohol and drug abusers, not those who currently use alcohol and drugs to excess. Thus, using the same logic, we would assume that if nicotine were classified as an addictive drug, only those who had quit smoking or were in a smoking "treatment" program would qualify for protection under ADA. So many employers now include smoking cessation clinics as part of an employee assistance program.

Regardless of the ADA, state laws forbidding discrimination against smokers are on the rise. These laws do not prevent employers from imposing office smoking bans or bans on smoking while in company vehicles. However, most do bar companies from refusing to hire smokers or firing employees who do not stop smoking. Some 28 states and the District of Columbia have smoker protections affecting hiring, firing, promotions, compensation, and /or occupational licensing.

Most of these states, but not all, allow higher insurance rates for smokers or allow wellness programs that reward workers for quitting or for not smoking. A few states with "smokers rights" legislation allow organizations whose mission is health promotion to hire only nonsmokers (e.g., Illinois and Rhode Island.)

Additional References:

Mook, Jonathan R. & Powell, Erin E. (1996). Substance abuse and the ADA: What every employer should know. *Employee Relations Law Journal*, Autumn,Vol.22, No.2, p.57-78.

Paul, Robert J. & Townsend, James B. (1998). Smoking in the workplace: Balancing smoker and nonsmoker rights. *Employee Responsibilities & Rights Journal*, Vol.11, No.2, p.117-133.

Ryan, James & Zwerling, Craig (1996). Cigarette smoking at hire as a predictor of employment outcome, *Journal of Occupational & Environmental Medicine*, Vol.38, p.928-933.

Soliciting fellow employees for fund-raisers

It may be wise to establish a policy to prevent this form of solicitation on company property. Many companies post "No Soliciting" signs, usually directed toward the individual vendor off-the-street.

However, if employee solicitation is occurring as frequently as you claim, you may want to broaden your message to include any and all forms of solicitation. Make sure to clearly state your position in your policy manual or via the company bulletin board. You may be hesitant to take action for fear of damaging employee morale. But we imagine there are quite a few members of your company who feel as bombarded as you do.

In addition, you wrote that you are able to say no when approached by one of your employees to purchase. However, can those employees who are approached by a teammate or their supervisor do the same? These employees may feel pressured to buy, concerned that saying no will damage peer relationships or even future organizational rewards. That certainly isn't good for morale either.

As a final piece of advice, it is recommended that any new policy or change should be clearly justified with your concerns and rationale included. In doing so, it is less likely that your actions will be misunderstood.

Additional References:

Ball, David (1998). I gave at work. *The Guardian*, June 29, p.1.

McCune, Jenny C. (1997). The corporation in the community. *HR Focus*, March, Vol.74, No.3, p.12-13.

Strategy & HRM

 One of most difficult challenges for the human resource manager is to become fully involved in an organization's strategic planning process rather than fill the role as implementer of top management's plan. Many organizations profess that they involve the HR department in strategy formation, but frustrated HR managers report that this commitment is not as widespread as it could be. In some organizations, this involvement is a constant struggle, but successes are being realized slowly.

A true strategic role will depend upon a recognition by the organization's senior management that its human capital—its people and their skills—goes a long way to providing a sustained competitive advantage for the company. But there are a few suggestions to help a new HR manager become more involved in the planning process.

The human resource manager must work well with numbers and give those numbers to top management in a language they can understand. Presenting a utility analysis to explain how important it is for the organization to buy personality and ability tests to use in the selection process may cause top management's eyes to glaze over. Reformulating that analysis to explain how it contributes to the organization's bottom line might catch the attention of the top managers. Many individuals who enter human resources stress that they are attracted by the people aspects of the job, but sometimes that just means they don't like math. These folks will find their careers short-circuited if they aren't comfortable working with numbers.

The people element *is* an important means to gain access to top management. It is an important step for the HR manager to cultivate powerful sponsors within the organization. Networking with top managers is crucial. One tactic used by a training manager at a growing community bank was a series of interviews with all top managers, surveying them on their training needs. These interviews—the first major task the training manager completed in her new job—formed the basis of a strategic training plan for the entire bank. Several of the managers she interviewed became champions for the plan.

One of your first activities should be in-depth discussions with top managers to determine what they want from human resources. You are a service operation, and these people are your customers. To better serve your customers, you must convince them that you need to be in on the planning process from the start.

After formulating a comprehensive HR plan based upon your discussions and your reading of the political forces within the organization, you should plan to keep in close contact with your internal customers. Networking, presenting relevant and understandable numbers, and projecting the fact that you expect to be involved in strategic planning are a few of the tactics that can be used to integrate HR into formulating strategy. Perhaps your predecessor was not aggressive enough in projecting her expectations of involvement, or did not delegate enough of the implementation to the rest of the HR staff. Let top management know you expect to be involved on the front end or there may be shortcomings in implementing the plan. Good luck.

Additional References:

Bennett, Nathan, Ketchen, David J. & Schultz, Elyssa B. (1998). An examination of factors associated with the integration of human resource management and strategic decision making. *Human Resource Management*, Vol.37, p.3-16.

Gubman, Edward L. (1996). The gauntlet is down. *Journal of Business Strategy*, Nov./Dec., Vol.17, No.6, p.33-35.

Succession planning

 Formally, succession planning means examining development needs given a firm's strategic plans. Informally, it means high-level managers identifying and developing their own replacements. There is no reason that we can think of for NOT having a succession planning process in your organization. Most companies have them, especially well-run ones. A small firm without such a plan may be more vulnerable than the larger firm, where knowledge and expertise are usually widely dispersed. Many small business owners shy away from succession planning for fear of recognizing that they won't always be in control of their business. Others are too caught up in the daily pressures of running a small business to plan for the future. A recent poll revealed that only about one-fourth of small business owners had succession plans, and only half of the one-fourth had committed the plan to paper. So you are not alone. In doing succession planning, small business owners should consider whether they want to keep the business in the family, recruit an outside manager to run it, sell it to a key employee, or put it on the market.

Succession planning is not only important for filling a spot in an emergency. The process of defining critical skills needed for leadership positions forces some strategic thinking among those who participate. That is, succession planning forces you to question what skills will be needed for a particular position in the future, and why succession plans are not "written in stone." There are still judgment and discretion required to replace leaders who become ill, die, or simply move on. But, if done correctly, the process itself has many benefits.

Additional References:

Brown, B. (1988). Succession strategies for family firms. *The Wall Street Journal*, Aug. 4, p. 23.

Walker, James (1998). Do we need succession planning anymore? *Human Resource Planning*, September, Vol.21, No.3, p9-11.

T

Team building

Although we often hear about the benefits of team building, as you have seen, the consequences often make things worse rather than better. On the positive side, most people enjoy being part of a close-knit, cohesive work group, participate more fully in group activities, more readily accept the group's goals, and are absent less often than members of less cohesive groups. Thus, we might expect that building a cohesive team that works well together also will yield high levels of performance.

However, building a cohesive team can only aid productivity when the supervisors and subordinates have the same goals and work together. A highly cohesive team may actually do great harm to an organization if the group's goals conflict with the organization's. In a group where workers get along well, they are more likely to agree with each other on what constitutes a "fair day's work." This leads group members to strive for and enforce that performance level.

Trying to change the group's perspective now that they are a solid team will be difficult. Before they will see eye-to-eye with you, a little anti–team building may be necessary. This may seem odd, but it is generally better to have a group divided when its values and goals are contrary to yours than it is to have the group unified against you. Anti–team building can be as simple as picking out one or two individuals and praising their performance instead of rewarding or praising the whole group. Not surprisingly, this is likely to create conflict on the team.

Once the break-up is complete, more positive steps must be taken to bring your views and the employees' views closer together and then rebuild the team. Anything that reinforces good performance (pay, perks, praise) and eliminates poor performance does the trick. Some managers get employees moving in the right direction by clarifying what is expected and giving a pep talk. Not every manager can do this well, but it can be very effective. Finally, it is important for you to be sensitive to the messages your actions may be sending to employees. For example, it should be obvious that if a manager wants to convince people to work long hours, the manager should not go home early.

Once you have the individual employees back on track, it is appropriate to team build again. This time, however, you will *all* be on the same team.

Additional References:

Carley, Mark S. (1996). Teambuilding: Lessons from the theater. *Training & Development*, August, Vol.5, No.8, p.41-43.

Donovan, Michael (1996). The first step to self-direction is not empowerment. *Journal for Quality & Participation*, June 1, Vol.19, No.3, p.64-66.

Glaser, Susan R. (1994). Teamwork and communication. *Management Communication Quarterly*, Vol.7, No.3, p.282-296.

Theft & forgiveness

 You are right to be concerned about the message you'd be sending to your ex-employee as well as your other employees: "It's OK to steal if the company is dependent upon you." Rather than hiring the employee back, we'd recommend that you concentrate your efforts on understanding why you can't find a replacement. Make certain you have examined your compensation level for that particular position and also your recruitment strategy. We're confident there are qualified applicants out in the market. However, you may be looking in the wrong places. In addition, there may be high demand for the particular skills you require, and your wages may not be competitive. Local compensation data for a variety of jobs are compiled by the U.S. Department of Labor, Bureau of Labor Statistics, and are available free of charge at the library.

Keep looking! When you find a replacement, we recommend that you cross-train several of your employees, so you are not faced with this dilemma in the future.

Additional References:

Cheraskin, Lisa & Campion, Michael A. (1996). Study clarifies job-rotation benefits. *Personnel Journal*, November, Vol.75, No.11, p.31-36.

Markels, Alex (1998). Is anybody out there? *Working Woman*, June, p.40-46.

Theft prevention

 Since you have no real proof that it was the ex-employee, you'll probably have little luck prosecuting anyone or recovering the stolen money. However, there are some actions you can take to prevent theft in the future.

Contrary to popular belief, small businesses actually have more problems with theft and fraud than larger businesses. The key reason lies in the fact that smaller businesses usually lack basic internal controls of the larger firms. In a firm your size, everyone's hands may be in the till. This is more likely in a small business, because there are usually less supervision and fewer checks or balances than in larger bureaucratic firms. These checks and balances usually include elaborate accounting and inventory management systems, or the segmenting of job responsibilities so that employees with the means to misappropriate money or merchandise lack the ability to hide it.

Additionally, many small business owners don't, but should, take an active role in monitoring the daily activities of the firm. The most popular bookkeeping software used by small businesses includes auditing functions that enable detection of unauthorized transaction deletions and other suspicious activity. The first action you should take is to run the audit regularly. Many owners turn off the audit function because its activation slows down the program, or they simply let audits slip through the cracks. Second, make certain that you personally open and examine bank statements and oversee accounting first-hand, looking for any unusual account activity.

In addition to establishing a paper trail and monitoring the firm's activities, you don't want to forget the front end: hiring those who are less prone to steal. Make certain that you sufficiently check references and backgrounds of the individuals you hire. There are also several inexpensive honesty/theft assessment tools that can be used to screen employees at the time of hiring.

Finally, studies have found that the manner in which a firm treats an employee is related to the level of theft in the organization. It has been found that an employee who is stealing from his employer often justifies it as "retribution for perceived injustices" (e.g., the employee feels unfairly treated or unfairly paid). Therefore it is important that you are perceived as being fair, open, and honest in dealing with your employees. Formal policies and procedures to ensure fairness, which are usually par for the course in larger firms, also should be present in your company.

Additional References:

Butler, Daniel (1999). Under surveillance: If employers are going to spot fraud in the workplace they've got to be vigilant - but they can go too far. *Accountancy*, April, p. 38-39.

Greenberg, Jerald (1990). Employee theft as a reaction to underpayment inequity: the hidden cost of pay cuts. *Journal of Applied Psychology*, October, Vol.75, No.5, p. 561-568.

Martin, Josh (1998). An HR guide to white collar crime. *HR Focus*, September, Vol.75, No.9, p. 1-3.

Tokenism

 Whether you complain about it depends on whether this remark represents a pattern of activity or just one isolated incident. It may be better to merely file the comment for future reference. Despite the staff person's apparent insensitivity to your feelings, we think that the corporate headquarters is inviting you to participate because you will bring unique talents and perspectives to the task force.

Joining the task force will give you an opportunity to discover whether the corporate people just want you there to pick your brain about your "group" or if they really want to take advantage of your broad range of skills as a valued employee. If the staff person's remark is true, it may be the former. If so, you will gain some information about the company that may help you make your long-term career plans. In other words, the corporate headquarters was dishonest with you when you were told you were invited to be on the task force based on your excellent work record. The headquarters staff had a hidden agenda. However, if you find that your insights are appreciated about all topics regarding the training needs of employees, you can evaluate the staff person's remark as a mere insult.

You also should keep in mind that in putting together task forces and committees such as this, it is in the company's business interest to make them as diverse as possible. This does not just mean from a racial standpoint, but also in terms of sex, age, work style, function or position within the company, skill level, and education level. These sorts of differences can be used to the organization's advantage when forming task forces or teams because it provides the company with a greater pool of knowledge about the organization, and it promotes creativity, innovation, and problem solving.

As an individual—with all of your experiences, talents, and characteristics—you bring a unique perspective to the group. This is based not merely on group memberships but also on your life experiences, personality, and education. You probably can provide a few insights concerning the training needs of multicultural employees, but we suspect you can provide information about a wide range of other issues. Being a member of the task force will enable you to do so.

Additional References:

Bond, Meg A. & Pyle, Jean L. (1998). The ecology of diversity in organizational settings: Lessons from a case study. *Human Relations,*Vol.51, p.589-623.

Carlton, Melinda & Hawkeye, Philip (1997). Affirmative action and affirming diversity: Has it been effective at the local level? *Public Management*, Vol.79, No.1, p.19-23.

Tongue rings & tattoos

Employees have filed suits against employers' dress and appearance codes under Title VII, usually claiming sex discrimination and even racial discrimination. However, most court cases involving dress, grooming, and hair requirements have been decided in favor of the employer. For example, Disney's rule against facial hair does not constitute sex discrimination because they only discriminate between clean-shaven and bearded men, a type of discrimination not qualified as sex bias under Title VII. Nor would letting women, but not men, wear earrings qualify, because this reflects a minor customary code of grooming. We can't imagine any way that body piercing would qualify.

However, before you give this employee an ultimatum, you should re-read the first sentence in your question: "I've got an employee who is a hard worker with a good attitude." Regardless of how offensive and disturbing you may find his appearance, you should ask yourself three questions: (1) Does his appearance interfere with the progress of the work being done? (2) Does his appearance interfere with fellow employees in their work? (3) Will his appearance damage the image, reputation, or services of the company? If you answer no to all three of these questions, your time is better spent dealing with legitimate problems.

Additional References:

Allred, Gloria, and Leal, Dolores Y. (1999). Employment; a "BFOQ" defense. *National Law Journal*, February, Vol.21, p.B8 col.1.

Anonymous (1996). Only in America. *Fortune*, June 24, Vol.133, No.12 , p.166.

Tuition reimbursement

 There are several reasons to provide tuition assistance to employees, other than helping the two of us stay gainfully employed. One of the more obvious benefits of a tuition reimbursement program is its place in your fringe benefits package. In addition to medical insurance, vacation, and sick leave, you are providing your employees with an extra that will do them good in the long term as well as the short term.

More than 70 percent of all American companies offer some sort of tuition reimbursement plan. Although tuition reimbursement is ranked by employees as one of their most valued benefits, according to a recent Hewitt Associates survey, it remains the most underused employee benefit.

As many employees have told us, they may not use the benefit, but having it available sends an important message about how the company feels toward them. It suggests to most that the company cares about its employees and is willing to make an investment in them.

For those who actually use the benefit, tuition assistance provides low-skill employees without a college degree the opportunity to make the transition into high-skilled work by getting specialized knowledge or a diploma.

For those working on an advanced degree, the courses enable further skills and knowledge required for successful transition into management ranks. Having the opportunity to make this transition reinforces the loyalty some employees have for the company and qualifies the employees for internal promotions.

It takes several years in some cases to complete a master's degree or undergraduate degree program on a part-time basis. You may be overlooking the fact that your employees come back to work from each class with knowledge that helps them perform their jobs more effectively. It has been our experience that most of the student/employees who return to school part time are highly motivated to succeed, both at work and at school.

Some of our best students have been full-time employees. These people know exactly what they want out of school and often apply this knowledge to their jobs. In many MBA courses, the students perform class projects that are directly focused on their current companies and jobs. The outcome of these projects has the potential to benefit the company. Students also learn problem solving, continuous learning, and interpersonal skills by working with others in groups. This knowledge is also applicable to the workplace.

Most importantly, tuition refund programs need to be tied to the employee's development program, which must be aligned with the organization's needs. The program should be designed and communicated to encourage business-related development and not to foster misuse.

As a manager, you need to be involved in the development plans of your employees. The tuition refund program provides a means for involvement, encouraging and guiding employees to obtain valuable business knowledge. If you take an interest in the employees' progress, you may get more out of these programs, and employees may feel more of an obligation to stay with the organization.

Although you express frustration when employees complete their degrees and leave, most employees pursuing work-related development are interested in continuing their careers with their current employer as long as the employer continues to provide challenges and career enhancement related to business needs. Perhaps that's why you've had the problem with turnover.

Additional References:

Baldwin, Timothy T. & Danielson, Camden (1997). The evolution of learning strategies in organizations: From employee development to business redefinition. *Academy of Management Executive*, November, Vol.11, No.4, p.47-58.

Tyler, Kathryn (1997). Expanded tuition policies save in the long run. *HRMagazine*, September, Vol.42., No.9, p.71-75.

Turnover

Many factors relating to individuals, their jobs, and economic conditions shape decisions to leave one organization for another, some of which you may have little ability to control. One way to establish if there is a pattern to the turnover and to affect those areas that are under your control is to conduct "exit interviews" with those employees who quit. Exit interviews can be difficult to conduct because it's hard to get departing employees to speak honestly for fear of "burning any bridges." Yet, when skillfully conducted and interpreted, exit interviews that focus on obtaining adequate rapport with the person leaving the job can produce useful results. For these reasons, having an external party conduct the interview is usually advised. Not only are employees more candid, but an external interviewer also brings impartiality, the ability to benchmark and interpret company-specific information with other employers, and the expertise to identify potential causes of the turnover problem. Of course, for the information obtained to be of real value, it should be combined, quantified, and analyzed across a number of interviews, rather than focusing on a single employee's comments.

Additional References:

Anonymous (1992). Turnover rates and costs. *Journal of Accountancy*, October, Vol.174, No.4, p.18.

Barada, Paul W. (1998). Before you go. *HR Magazine*, December, Vol.43, p.99-102.

Shaw, Jason D., Delery, John E., Jenkins, G. Douglas, Jr., & Gupta, Nina (1998). An organization-level analysis of voluntary and involuntary turnover. *Academy of Management Journal*, October, Vol.41, No.5, p.511-525.

U

Unemployment Compensation

Based on what you've described, it is unlikely the employee could win her case in court. Many states follow the common-law doctrine of employment-at-will. The employment-at-will principle assumes that employers are generally free to terminate the employment relationship at any time—and without notice—for any reason, no reason, or even a bad reason. Of course, this assumes that the individual is not terminated due to race, sex, religion, or other federally protected classifications and that there is no employment contract, actual or implied.

As for unemployment benefits, her immediate termination by you may make her eligible. If she does apply and receives compensation, the amount of your organization's future contributions to the unemployment insurance fund may be affected. Remember, your company's unemployment tax is determined by the extent to which it has contributed to the unemployment roll. However, when submitting her application for unemployment compensation, she also must register for available work and be willing to accept any suitable employment she may be offered by the state employment agency. Given that she is leaving your company to start her own business, it seems unlikely she would take this course of action.

Yet, anybody can sue for anything. In addition, you may prevail in court but lose valuable time, legal fees, and energy in the process. We believe it is important to keep an employee's exit from an organization as fair and amicable as possible for all parties concerned. When exit from an organization is handled with fairness in mind, the negative outcomes about which you are concerned (taking your client base or taking you to court) are very unlikely. Even when terminating a poorly performing employee, showing personal consideration, being honest and tactful, and treating the individual with dignity will increase the perception of fair treatment and lessen the potential for employee retaliation. Your reactions of anger and feeling betrayed are certainly normal. However, your reactions likely will lead to the outcomes you don't want. Get control of your emotions and remember the words of Winston Churchill: "If you have to kill a man, it costs nothing to be polite."

Because she was one of your best employees and she will now be one of your competitors, we recommend that you accept her resignation, pay her two weeks' severance, and have her leave the premises today.

Additional References:

Brown, Marc E. (1998). When employees leave. *Electronic Business*, June, Vol.24, No.6, p. 43.

Lisoski, Ed (1998). How to terminate an employee with their dignity intact and you out of the courts. *Supervision*, May, Vol.59, No.5, p.7-9.

Olson, Walter K. (1997). *The excuse factory: How employment law is paralyzing the American workplace*. New York: The Free Press.

Union comfort level

 Asking specifically about previous experience in a union shop would be the worst way to obtain the information you want. Rather, you should design questions that attempt to discover whether the prospective employee has the *skills* needed to succeed in your organization's labor environment. If your organization stresses teamwork between labor and management, you should ask applicants about their skills in working as members of a team. If your organization has a more adversarial relationship between labor and management, you should focus your questions on the applicant's ability to cope in that environment.

Merely asking about previous experience in a union shop does not provide you with any information about how that person will get along in *your* union shop. When you ask for an applicant's employment history, you will get this information anyway, without being seen as probing for information that is irrelevant to job performance. And if you do not hire the applicant, the applicant could file an unfair labor practice complaint claiming that you did not hire him because he was a union member. (See "Salting.")

About 20 states, mainly in the South and West, are right-to-work states where union membership cannot be made a condition of employment. Asking questions about prior employment in union shops could be construed by the applicant as putting pressure on the applicant to join the union. In those states, the union will be happy to apply this pressure in subtle ways after the person has been hired.

Additional References:

Foegen, Joseph H. (1998). The `devil theory' one more time. *Employee Responsibilities & Rights Journal*, Vol.11, p.57-63.

Moore, William J. (1998). The determinants and effects of right-to-work laws: A review of the recent literature. *Journal of Labor Research*, Vol.19, p.445-468.

Saltzman, Gregory M. (1995). Job applicant screening by a Japanese transplant: A union-avoidance tactic. *Industrial & Labor Relations Review*, Vol.49, p. 88-104.

V

Violence at work

The Bureau of Labor Statistics has released reports in recent years identifying homicide as one of the leading causes of death in the workplace. In addition, the Justice Department's Bureau of Justice Statistics said in 1998 that about two million people a year were victims of violent crime or threatened violent crime in the workplace from 1992 to 1996. Four years earlier, the Justice Department found that one million workers a year were victims of nonviolent workplace crimes. With many companies fearful, workplace violence has become a "Golden Cow" for many consultants, authors, and seminar speakers.

However, a closer look at the studies suggests that violence attributed to disgruntled workers is actually very rare. For example, in 1994, only 59 on-the-job or on-duty killings were attributed to co-workers or an ex-employee. In 1995, on-the-job violence figures dramatically increased due to those federal workers killed on duty in the Oklahoma City bombing.

There are two main reasons workplace violence has become such a hot issue and a confusing one. First, workplace violence can be likened to a plane crash. There may be few incidences, but when they occur, they scare the pants off you due to sensational media coverage. Witness coverage of post office shootings, Oklahoma City, killings at public schools in the last two years, and the murders of the two on-duty police officers inside the U.S. Capitol in July1998.

Second, recent studies have defined workplace violence so broadly that it has become ordinary violence under a new name. In addition, the 1998 Justice figures included threat of violence, which doubles the number of incidents from one million to two million.

Virtually every study of workplace violence includes any attack that occurs on company property or while the victim was on duty, regardless of whether the crime was related to work or not. Those most at risk (based on incidents per 1,000 workers), according to the Justice figures, are law enforcement officers, private security guards, cab drivers, prison or jail guards, and bartenders! Mental health professionals, gas

166

station attendants, convenience store clerks, mental health workers, and middle school teachers rounded out the top 10. These workers are not at risk because of a violent co-worker or an employment issue, but because of the hazards of dealing with the customers of their chosen occupation.

Excluding these occupations, it has been found that most of the violence, which ranged from threats of assault to rape, occurred in parking lots, in garages, or even on public property (such as streets and parks) while the employee was on duty.

Yet, violence against co-workers can become a problem particularly in instances where restructuring has occurred, when an employee is under heavy stress, or when an employee has recently been terminated or demoted. Warning signs that serious violence might occur include threatening remarks from employees, temper tantrums, and cantankerous behavior. Take all threats seriously.

As an employer, you should take steps to ensure that you are doing all you can to prevent violent acts from occurring on the job. Some possible preventive measures include a written policy that explains the organization's stance on violent behavior and establishes a procedure for investigating threats against co-workers, a plan developed in conjunction with security specialists, counselors, and law enforcement for dealing with violent incidents.

Show sensitivity to the needs of those who are victims of layoffs, those involved in some other major organizational change, or those who require discipline. Perhaps key to this sensitivity is keeping employees informed about impending changes and providing some sort of support so they can more readily adjust to the change. Hire carefully by checking all of the applicants' background information for a history of problems. There are also psychological tests that, when properly administered, can reveal an individual's propensity for violence.

Additional References:

Coco, Malcolm P. (1998). The new war zone: The workplace. *S.A.M. Advanced Management Journal,* , Winter, Vol.63, No.1, p.15-20.

Paul, Robert J. & Townsend, James B. (1998). Violence in the workplace—a review with recommendations. *Employee Responsibilities and Rights Journal,* Vol.11, p.1-15.

Schaner, Dean J. (1996). Have gun, will carry: Concealed handgun laws, workplace violence and employer liability. *Employee Relations Law Journal,* Summer, Vol.22. No.1, p.83-101.

Weather, storms, & natural disasters

There are a variety of ways to handle this situation, particularly if you do not have an inclement weather policy. (And considering how mild winters are in many southern states, your company may not have one.) One method to handle compensation after a weather emergency is to have a policy to pay those employees who reported to work a full day's pay and to have those who could not report or left early use vacation or personal time—if they have any—for the time they did not work. Otherwise, they would not be paid for the hours missed.

However, because an ice storm may be rare in your area and the above-mentioned policy was not in force, you may want to pay all employees for the day and then put your policy into effect for future incidents. If some employees worked during the inclement weather and others did not, you may want to provide those who worked with two personal days off to be fair to those who came to work. An added incentive such as time and a half for hourly employees might be appropriate for those who worked. Salaried employees would be paid regardless, but those who made it to work might be rewarded with extra merit pay for turning out and doing what needed to be done that day. Take care in making sure that your decision is perceived as equitable to both salaried as well as hourly employees.

Whatever your decision regarding pay, you should realize that it may have a great impact on how your employees view your organization. If you want to reinforce your company's values as a caring company, you should do what you can to be fair to all of your employees under these difficult circumstances, even if it costs the company some money, because your decision may have future repercussions.

When presented with this question, one of us recalled a former employer who docked all employees a day's pay if they were unable to come to work during a great blizzard in the north several years ago. The CEO's actions became a standard example whenever employees discussed how cheap and unreasonable the firm was toward its workers. When the CEO retired, the employees presented skits satirizing him as a major skinflint because of his actions during the weather emergency. From his perspective, he viewed his actions as an effort to be fair to all of the employees, those who came to work and those who could not. But the employees made their own judgments about what was fair.

Additional References:

Milbank, Dana & Duff, Christina (1996). Blizzard, budget battle are no match for determined government employees. *Wall Street Journal*, January 11, Vol.227, No.8, p.A16.

Wortham, Sarah (1997). Expect the unexpected: How to protect your workers in a natural disaster. *Safety & Health*, September, Vol.156, No.3, p.48-54.

Work relationships & "getting along"

You terminated an individual who had bad working relations with leaders in her area, who could not handle multiple tasks or work in your organization's team. To us, the rationale for your decision was quite clear, and the action justifiable. As you witnessed, good overall job performance usually involves much more than good technical skills. Aside from technical ability, do the individual's desires, interests, and perspectives mesh with the organization's practices and procedures? If not, the person may not be a good fit with your organization's culture. Think of an individual whose philosophy of management assumes that employees will only work hard when they are pushed or goaded into performing (i.e., because there is a carrot at the end of the stick) and who feels employees need strong direction from their leaders at all times. This hypothetical individual probably wouldn't last very long in a highly participative, or team-oriented, company.

Improved selection procedures that take into consideration the job characteristics, organizational culture, and individual attributes may prevent an unsuccessful hiring decision in the future. You also may want to incorporate a realistic job preview (RJP) into your recruitment/hiring process. RJPs should provide a clear picture of what the job entails and a general "feel" for organizational practices. This enables candidates to evaluate how comfortable they feel they will be working for your organization. You may lose a few candidates in the process. However, your voluntary and involuntary turnover, caused by "bad fit," also should decline.

Additional References:

Cable, Danial M. & Judge, Timothy A. (1997). Interviewers' perceptions of person-organization fit and organizational selection decisions. *Journal of Applied Psychology, August,* Vol.82, No.4, p.546-562.

Hirshman, Carolyn (1998). Playing the high stakes hiring game. *HRMagazine,* March, Vol.43, No.4, p. 80-86

Perian, John (1996). The emotionally impaired. *Supervision*, Nov., Vol.57, No.11, p.3-5.

Roth, P. G., Roth, P. L. (1995). Reduce turnover with realistic job previews. *The CPA Journal*, September, Vol.65, No.9, p.68-69.

"X" generation

 Articles and recent concerns about managing the so-called "X" generation reflect the increased diversity of the workforce, the tight labor market, and the understanding by organizations that the best way to gain a competitive edge is through the individual employee. Responding to the wants and needs of the employees and figuring out how employees are motivated and what rewards and working conditions are desired are all crucial to organizational success and to achieving competitive advantage.

The generation "X" employees, born between 1965 and 1976, seem to have different values than the "baby boomers" born between 1942 and 1964. "Baby boom" managers are attempting to understand how "X" generation workers differ from themselves at work because of these value differences. Not so long ago, organizations were attempting to understand how to best supervise the idiosyncratic "baby boom" generation. It is a never-ending process.

"X" generation employees, also called the "baby bust" generation, have certainly been on the wrong end of some unflattering stereotypes. "Gen X" employees have been stereotyped as being angry and bitter, lacking in work ethic, having a short attention span, and being less loyal to their companies. These stereotypes are about as valid as labeling all "boomers" as idealistic ,warm-hearted hippies. In our opinion, managers who attempt to act on the basis of these stereotypes are wrong to do so, just as they would be wrong to act on unfounded stereotypes based on race or sex.

Interestingly, in 1994, a survey by Kenneth Kovach of George Mason University found that people of different ages *do* have different work priorities. For example, workers ages 31–40, a mix of "gen x" and "boomer", had the following top five priorities: (1) job security, (2) interesting work, (3) full appreciation of work done, (4) being involved in decisions, and (5) good wages. Workers under 30, and at that time representing "gen x", had these five priorities: (1) good wages, (2) job security, (3) promotion and growth within the company, (4) interesting work, and (5) full appreciation of the work done. Finally, "boomers", ages 41–50, had these top priorities: (1) being involved in decisions, (2) full appreciation of the work done, (3) interesting work, (4) job security, and (5) good wages.

So, how do we gain insight into the management of these diverse groups without inappropriately stereotyping individuals? We suggest generalizing about people's priorities and then building specific programs to meet the needs of individual employees. Take, for example, the generalization of working women. Not all working women are concerned about balancing family and work life, but many are. Starting from the stereotypical premise that women take a more active role in child care than do men, the organization might take steps to tailor benefit packages that appeal to women and address this child care need. This stereotype does not apply to all female employees, but it is a starting point to address individual needs. The same is true with generalizations and stereotypes of "boomers" and "X" generation employees.

Related References:

Woodward, N. H. (1999). The coming of the x manager. *HRMagazine*, March, Vol.44, No.3, p.75-80.

Zemke, Ron (1999). Generation gaps in the classroom. *Training*, November, Vol.36, No.11, p.48-54.

X & Y management

 Of course, it is possible that your old manager was inflating employee performance scores. Similarly, your new manager may be overly strict with his ratings. However, the differing perceptions of these two managers, as well as the different results they obtained from their employees, also may be attributed to each of their contrasting views about human nature. Your previous office manager seems to have "Theory Y" assumptions toward human behavior, and the current manager seems to exemplify "Theory X" views.

More than 35 years ago, Douglas McGregor used the terms Theory X and Theory Y to describe different assumptions people make about those they supervise at work. McGregor's book—*The Human Side of Enterprise*—critiqued traditional approaches to management and offered a broader perspective on potential management techniques.

In brief, the Theory X manager stresses a traditional approach to directing and controlling employees. The Theory X manager assumes that the average person is lazy, dislikes work, and will avoid it if possible. Therefore, the manager believes that coercion, control, direction, and threats work best to convince the employees to put forth effort on their jobs. The Theory X manager believes employees value security above all and will respond to the techniques practiced by the manager so they can stay employed. Although this approach sounds rather draconian, it served as a basis for organizational supervision for centuries, and still does in many organizations.

On the other hand, Theory Y assumptions include the idea that working is just as natural as play, external threats are not the best way to stimulate effort, getting rewards leads people toward achieving goals, and the average person seeks responsibility rather than avoids it. These points may seem obvious and are practiced by many companies today through the use of employee involvement and empowerment and job enrichment. But when McGregor published his book, the Theory Y assumptions were considered somewhat revolutionary. In practice, the Theory Y view encourages employees to take responsibility, make decisions, and get involved in their work. This approach increases employee involvement and interest in the job, but sometimes the Theory Y manager may be let down by an employee who merely wants to take advantage.

What is troubling about Theory X assumptions is that employees may start behaving the way the manager expects them to behave. If your supervisor treats employees as though they are lazy and do not want to work, his assumptions and expectations may become reality.

You may find it useful to explore, with your manager, his general assumptions and expectations regarding any employee's performance. For example, how did he treat his staff prior to coming on board with you? You also may want to point out the message he may have sent his staff since his first day on the job. Numerous studies have found that a manager's expectations and treatment of subordinates largely determine the subordinates' performance. Subordinates, more often than not, do what they believe they are expected to do.

In George Bernard Shaw's *Pygmalion*, Eliza Doolittle explains: "The difference between a lady and a flower girl is not how she behaves but how she's treated. I shall always be a flower girl to Professor Higgins because he always treats me as a flower girl and always will . . . but I know I can be a lady to you because you always treat me as a lady and always will."

Related References:

Dvir, Taly & Eden, Dov (1995). Self-fulfilling prophecy and gender: Can women be Pygmalion and Galatea? *Journal of Applied Psychology*, Vol.80, p.253-270.

Lee, Chris & Zemke, Ron (1993). The search for spirit in the workplace. *Training*, June, Vol.30, No.6, p.21-27.

Neuliep, James W. (1996). The influence of theory X and Y management style on the perception of ethical behavior in organizations. *Journal of Social Behavior & Personality*, Vol.11, p.301-311.

Rheem, Helen (1995). Effective leadership. *Harvard Business Review*, May/June Vol.73, No.3, p.14-17.

Xenophobia

One of the major criteria that companies use in selecting managers for international assignments is technical abilities. These abilities include administrative skills, knowledge of the company's home operations, managerial talent, and technical expertise. A survey by International Orientation Resources indicated that 90 percent of all companies base international assignments on the applicant's technical expertise, while another 64 percent also assess a candidate's managerial ability. Patrick seems to fit the bill in those technical categories and probably would make a good choice based on those limited criteria.

However, to have a successful experience with your new manager in this sensitive position, it would be wise to look at other factors before you make this decision. In addition to technical abilities, an individual selected for an international assignment should possess relational skills (including empathy for the new culture, flexibility, ability to communicate across cultures, and knowledge of foreign language), an adaptable family situation, and motivation to work overseas, particularly within the specific culture of the host country. From what you have indicated about Patrick, he can speak the language but holds some level of contempt for the country where he would be sent. This appears to be a recipe for failure because he would have to work closely with people from a culture that he apparently does not like. In many cases, organizations send the most technically qualified person into another country only to have the individual fail because relational skills, family situation, or motivation were lacking.

Patrick seems to possess a heavy dose of ethnocentrism, bordering on xenophobia. Ethnocentrism is the belief that one's own culture is superior to other cultures and xenophobia is a fear of foreign people. Patrick's talk around the office could even result in discrimination actions on the part of Hispanic employees before he is sent on any international assignment. Thus, we would suggest counseling him on his office comments, ensure that he does not make further disparaging comments on the job, and determine the reasons behind those comments.

An effort at educating Patrick in cultural diversity might be called for if only to head off the possibility of lawsuits stemming from actions he takes in his current position. Diversity training might even provide him with an intercultural awareness that would suit him for future international assignments. For this particular job, you should widen the candidate pool.

Related References:

Darlington, Gerry (1996). Culture: A theoretical review. In Joynt, Pat & Warner, Malcolm (Eds.), *Managing across cultures: Issues and perspectives* (p.33-55), London: International Thomson Business Press.

Spreitzer, Gretchen M., McCall, Morgan W. Jr., & Mahoney, Joan D. (1997). Early identification of international executive potential, *Journal of Applied Psychology*, Vol.82, p.6-29.

"Yellow dog" contract

The only reason we can fathom for the owner to ask you to sign what is termed a "yellow dog" contract is ignorance of the fact that she is violating a federal labor law that was passed way back in 1932. Contracts that require nonunion membership as a condition of employment were made unenforceable by the Norris-LaGuardia Act. Such working conditions constitute unfair labor practices under subsequent federal labor laws because they interfere with the employees' right to organize.

Obviously, the company is very eager to stop employee efforts to unionize and, if they are aware of the law, they may think they can intimidate younger workers into believing that by signing a paper, they are giving up their rights to unionize. Federal laws do permit states to pass right-to-work laws, which forbid forcing employees to join a union to keep their jobs. These laws are in effect in about 20 states. However, it is illegal for employees to be forced to sign contracts that say they will not join a union.

There are much better—and legal—tactics that can be used by companies seeking to stay nonunion. The first tactic is for the company to set up fair discipline policies, open communication between managers and employees, and fair salaries and benefits. A second tactic is to attempt to detect union organizing as early as possible. One way to do this is to train first-line supervisors to look for changes in employee behavior and signs of union activity such as literature or authorization cards. If the union is able to attract enough interest to result in a federally supervised union election, the company should present its case to stay nonunion strongly and repeatedly through speeches to employees, informal meetings, and letters to employees. It would be wise for the company to seek legal counsel in planning a strategy to stay union free because federal labor laws provide many safeguards to protect the employees' rights to organize. Unions take full advantage of these mechanisms to file unfair labor practice complaints against employers with the National Labor Relations Board.

Any employer who would try to force its employees to sign away their rights probably wouldn't be following effective tactics to stay union free anyway. Therefore, your restaurant is probably a prime target for union organizers, which are trying to unionize service businesses more aggressively than they have in the past.

Related References:

Featherman, Mark (1996). Mandatory arbitration agreements as an unfair labor practice. *Labor Law Journal*, March, Vol.47, No.3, p.162-178.

Jenero, Kenneth & Spognardi, Mark A. (1996). Defending against the corporate campaign: Selected legal responses to common union tactics. *Employee Relations Law Journal*, Autumn, Vol.22, No.2, p.119-139.

Z

Zero defects

The actions of the president as you describe them raise a number of important issues. These issues include the important distinction between real and stated goals, the need for top management support to make new programs work, and the relationship between zero defects and costs.

Many times top managers of organizations make lofty official statements to the public, customers, and employees. These stated goals are what the managers want their employees and customers to believe are the objectives. However, what they really want to achieve can be better observed by looking at what they actually do. As a wise sage once stated, "People may not believe what you say, but they will always believe what you do." What organizations actually do reveals their real goals.

Your president perhaps believes that "zero-defects culture" is what customers and employees want to hear, rather than cost cutting—his real goal. On the other hand, your president may be just a bit confused as to the relationship between a zero-defects culture and cost cutting.

Much of the popular press, addressing zero-defects cultures obtained through continuous quality improvement, define CQI or TQM as a "people-focused system that aims at continual increases in customer satisfaction at continually lower real costs." At first glance, one might say your president is doing exactly that—raising the quality and cutting the budget. However, the lower real costs to which the definition refers are realized in the long run, not in the short run through budget cuts.

If top management at the company really wants to establish a zero-defects culture, it must invest in training its workers to perform each other's jobs, to make important operating decisions, and to identify processes that will increase quality and profitability.

The employees must develop the skills to examine their manufacturing or service processes with an eye to determining where defects occur and how to eliminate them. The company must reward employees for quick response to customer needs.

When it has become second nature among employees to serve the customer through zero defects, the president will see dramatic cost reductions in waste, defective products, and returned products. And sales should go in the opposite direction from costs.

Finally, for a zero-defects program, or any large-scale change program, to work, a key element is active and strong leadership from the top manager. Many quality programs such as those your president discussed have failed to be implemented properly because the organization's top leadership was not fully behind them, not willing to provide the material and inspirational resources for them to succeed.

In fact, many quality programs have failed because the organization attempted to restructure and downsize its work force (i.e., cut costs) at the same time it was asking its employees to take a greater role in making decisions on the shop floor. It's up to top management to take actions consistent with its vision if it wants to achieve zero defects. If this commitment is shown, the key players in making quality programs and zero-defects cultures work—middle management and rank-and-file employees—will buy into the programs and implement them more successfully.

Related References:

Anand, K.N. (1996). Quality strategy for the 1990s--the key is middle management. *Total Quality Management*, Vol.7, p.411-420.

Choi, Thomas Y. & Behling, Orlando (1997). Top managers and TQM success: One more look after all these years, *The Academy of Management Executive*, February, Vol.11, No.1, p.37-47.

theft, 23, 53, 102, 103, 158, 159

Title VII, 26, 30, 45, 48, 53, 54, 93, 101, 118, 144, 160

total quality management, 15, 43, 63, 176

training, 1, 3, 4, 7, 11, 16, 19, 20, 30, 37, 52, 53, 57, 68, 76, 89, 90, 92, 98, 113, 128, 134, 135, 138, 139, 140, 154, 159, 160, 174, 176

trust, 35, 43, 124, 133, 142

tuition reimbursement programs, 55, 140, 161, 162

turnover, 22, 27, 41, 55, 112, 128, 138, 145, 146, 162, 163, 169, 170

unemployment insurance, 56, 164

union, 44, 47, 56, 57, 62, 87, 93, 148, 149, 165, 175

unsafe, 3, 30, 37, 68, 87

validity, 23, 41, 90, 110

values, 11, 73, 80, 110, 111, 144, 156, 168, 170

violence, 5, 17, 30, 40, 57, 166, 167

Wagner Act, 62

work relationships, 20

workers' compensation, 3, 34, 37

wrongful discharge, 14, 56, 87

"X"-generation, 59, 112, 170

"yellow dog" contracts, 62, 174

zero defects, 62, 176